KU-755-624

CONTENTS

PREFACE

THERE was a time when mention of keeping fishes as pets at once brought to the mind of the average person a picture of goldfish in a glass globe. Nowadays the keeping of the gorgeously coloured tiny tropical fishes in the home has gained so many devotees, and tropical aquaria have become so widely used as decorative furnishings for hotel lounges, restaurants, shops and elsewhere, that their ubiquity has made the goldfish-and-bowl picture out of date. However, the goldfish retains its popularity despite this competition, and since records of its domestication can be traced to as far back as the tenth century it can truly be said to be among man's oldest-established pets.

In *Aquariums*,[1] a companion volume to this present handbook, a special chapter was devoted to the goldfish as a deserving case for such preferential treatment. It soon became obvious from correspondence that readers whose sole interest was the goldfish required more extensive and detailed information about this species to be made available, and the following pages are my endeavour to meet their request. If the gaps in our knowledge concerning the cultivation of fish in ponds and aquaria which are pointed out in the text tempt those who take their hobby seriously to make their own investigations, yet another justification for this book will be found.

I am very happy to record sincere thanks to my good friend, Mr. A. Boarder, well known as a practical goldfish breeder and authoritative judge of goldfish varieties, who has kindly contributed an informative chapter on exhibiting fish at shows.

[1]*Aquariums*, by Anthony Evans.   ANTHONY EVANS

CHAPTER 1

COLDWATER AQUARIUM-KEEPING

BECAUSE under normal circumstances there is a free and abundant supply of air for the use of captive animals in cages or other enclosures, little special thought is usually given to this aspect of their welfare by their keepers. With adequate ventilation no troubles arise from interference with the essential process of respiration when quite large groups of terrestrial animals are brought together in captivity, but with aquatic animals such as fishes, disastrous are the consequences of overlooking their respiratory requirements.

In common with all other living creatures, fishes require oxygen. This they obtain from the water in which they live by means of their gills, and the origin of the oxygen in water is the atmosphere. Since the process of solution of the gas from air requires a little time if the water is static, if in a tank there is a rate of uptake of oxygen from the water which exceeds this low rate of replacement from the air, it is obvious that oxygen starvation will soon be experienced by living occupants of the tank.

SHAPE OF THE AQUARIUM

To secure the best possible replacement of oxygen in the water it must either be agitated constantly or else exposed to the atmosphere in a thin layer—so that its surface area is maximal. For example, the surface formed by water in a filled milk bottle does not permit gases of the air to dissolve in the water very rapidly; if this water is tipped into a large soup plate, however, its surface is then very large in relation to its volume and rapid solution of air can occur. Containers for fishes must follow this pattern. They must allow the water within them to form a large surface, but not be too deep. There are offered for sale many different sizes of aquaria all having these desired proportions.

Because goldfish are relatively large fishes their rate of oxygen

7

consumption is rather high, and for this reason and the one that large fish require a generous allowance of swimming space, aquaria for goldfish should be selected from the larger sizes available. Unless the fishes are to be kept singly, aquaria of less than nine gallons capacity (size eighteen inches long by twelve inches by twelve inches) are of little use for goldfish keepers. A very useful-sized aquarium is the fifteen gallons tank (twenty-four inches long, twelve inches wide and fifteen inches deep). The number of fishes such a tank will contain without causing distress from respiratory difficulties obviously depends upon their size, and fish capacity of aquaria is considered later on in this chapter.

An aquarium needs to be more than just a container for water and fish, however. If it is to be a permanent home for the fish additional furnishings in the shape of sand and water plants are necessary. These transform the bare tank to something more approaching the natural surroundings and create an ornamental effect. Moreover, they play their part in maintaining the purity of the water, and in this way reduce the amount of work the fish-keeper has to do to ensure the continued health of his charges. Stages to be followed in preparing the 'furnished aquarium' are listed in the following paragraphs.

AQUARIUM FURNISHING

1. *Selection of Site.*—Small aquaria for goldfish should be placed under cover where there is no risk of the water in them freezing solid in cold weather. Aquaria require strong supports, for the weight of their contents is considerable: each gallon of water weighs over ten pounds, and to the weight of the water is to be added that of the sand. A strong wooden table can be made to take the aquarium, or an angle-iron stand can be purchased specially for the purpose. The stand should be at least four feet high so that the aquarium can be viewed in comfort, and it should be a rigid structure to reduce the transmission of vibrations or shocks.

Where the stand is to be placed will be dictated largely by available illumination. Light is necessary for the growth of water plants, so that unless electric lighting is provided in the way described later on, a position close to a window usually has to be selected. However, it is undesirable for the tank to receive the full glare of the summer afternoon sun, and the vicinity of a north or north-east facing window forms the ideal site.

2. *Bottom Media.*—For water plant growing a layer of sand is used on the tank bottom. In it plants form roots which anchor them in position. Sand obtained from a river bed, sieved to remove large stones, is ideal. Coarse sands are better than very fine ones for goldfish tanks, but the sand particles should not be so large that the layer forms a trap for fish foods and droppings to collect and putrefy and foul the water. For this reason gravel is an unsuitable bottom medium for the aquarium.

Before using the sand it must be thoroughly washed or else the water in the tank will never be clear. If sand direct from a river is used scald it with boiling water several times after washing it free from fine particles. Even the so-called 'already-washed' sand obtained from aquatic suppliers needs some washing to remove the dust which collects in it during transport and storage. A small sample of sand will not, after proper washing, cause any cloudiness when shaken with water in a jam-jar.

The washed sand is layered on the tank base to give a depth of about one inch at the front glass, and arranged to slope up to a depth of nearly three inches at the back of the aquarium. About twenty-four pounds of sand will be found adequate to layer a twenty-four inch aquarium in this way.

3. *Rocks.*—Rocks are used in goldfish aquaria solely for decorative effect. Two or three small pieces are all that is advisable for the fifteen-gallons aquarium, and they should be selected to be free from sharp protrusions. Only hard stones can be used—avoid limestone, marble or crystalline formations. Pieces of black coal may be used with effect, but as with other rocks these should be well scrubbed before use. Set the rocks in position in the sand layer, burying their bases in this so that no crevices exist beneath them.

4. *Water.*—When the sand and rocks are in position water should be added to the aquarium until it is two-thirds full. If it is poured in carefully on to a saucer or a sheet of brown paper placed temporarily on the sand surface the slope of the layer will

not be disturbed. Water from the domestic mains is used for aquaria, unless it is delivered from copper pipes or is very hard 'chalky' water. Hard waters can be diluted with rain water from a clean butt or with distilled water, using equal volumes of each. Chlorine in the water supply is not usually in sufficient amount to cause trouble, but if there is any doubt leave the water to stand in a bath for several hours before using it.

5. *Water Plants and Planting.*—Many of the water plants used in aquaria are propagated by cuttings, and they are supplied in this form by traders. They root readily when placed in the aquarium, and several cuttings of each kind of plant can be bunched together with a thread tie or a loop of lead wire at the lower ends of the stems. These ends are then pushed beneath the sand where the plants are to take root. Other plants are supplied entire—that is, complete with roots. These can be set in groups but should not be bunched, and only the rooted part must be buried in the sand. Planting is most easily done by pushing the stems down into the water with a stick having a U-shaped notch cut in one end while another stick is employed to bury the ends or the roots in the sand.

Of the many plants available for coldwater aquarium use the ones mentioned here are the most easily obtainable and are specially suited to the goldfish tank. *Vallisneria*, which always has its roots when purchased, is rather like a grass in appearance and will form a good background screen for the aquarium. Similar to it is *Sagittaria*, and another rooted plant with very fine leaves described by its name is hair grass (*Eleocharis*). *Egeria densa* is obtained as cuttings, and so are milfoil (*Myriophyllum*), water violet (*Hottonia palustris*), hornwort (*Ceratophyllum*), *Ludwigia* and willow moss (*Fontinalis antipyretica*).

For an aquarium twenty-four inches long about three dozen plants and cuttings suffice to give a well-planted effect. As mentioned before, the cuttings are planted in bunches of four or five stems, and if lead wire is not used to keep them together and submerged, a few pebbles may be placed on the sand about their stems to stop them from rising. The arrangement of the plants in the tank should be done carefully, and it is usual to dispose the bulk of the plants at the ends and at the back of the tank so as to leave the

Fig. 1. Aquarium water plants—
Vallisneria, Myriophyllum, hair grass.

Fig. 2. Aquarium water plants—
Egeria densa, water violet, hornwort.

Fig. 3. Aquarium water plants—
Ludwigia, willow moss, *Sagittaria.*

front area clear. The positions in which the plants give the best effect will be found only by trying them in different places and viewing the result each time through the front glass. It is for this reason that planting is done with water in the aquarium, for although an empty aquarium can be planted it is more difficult to judge what the effect will be whilst planting is in progress.

Unfortunately it is not always easy to maintain the well arranged and fully planted state of the goldfish aquarium because of the fondness of goldfish for fresh green food. Their habits of eating the leaves and constantly scavenging in the sand at the bottom permit only the faster-growing and tougher plants to survive, and they are often uprooted. Setting the plants in a bank of sand kept in position by a vertical sheet of glass about four inches from the back of the aquarium is one way of overcoming this, and it is often the case that as soon as the plants have grown and rooted well, when the glass is removed they are better able to withstand rough treatment by the fishes. The glass cannot be seen when it is beneath the water and does not spoil the tank's appearance.

6. *Aquarium Cover.*—A sheet of glass to form a cover for the aquarium is necessary to prevent the deposition of dust on the water surface and to reduce the loss of water by evaporation. Short pieces of rubber tubing, slit along their lengths and slipped over the edge of the aquarium frame at various points around its top will raise the glass enough to admit air and will also prevent water from collecting between glass and frame.

If electric lighting is to be used for the aquarium—and in Britain the amount of natural light penetrating indoors is insufficient for sustained plant growth six months in the year—then a cover can be made for the top of the aquarium to house the lamps, or the ready-made article may be purchased. The lamps must be well away from the water surface or else their heating effect will influence the aquarium temperature. For an aquarium near a window the lights need only be on during dark days, and for a twenty-four inch aquarium in such a position one forty-watt bulb or strip light will probably be found adequate. Goldfish will not in the least mind a strong overhead light, but strong lighting from the side is both unpleasant for fish and the cause of uneven plant growth.

There is no need to provide heating for goldfish aquaria, and the average living-room temperature of 60° F. suits them admirably. It should be noted that warm water will hold less oxygen than cold, so that if the aquarium temperature does rise on a very hot day the fishes will show signs of oxygen shortage by swimming listlessly and mouthing at the water surface. For some of the fancy varieties it may be necessary to provide a gentle heat in winter if the aquarium is in a cold situation, but this is discussed in the section dealing with these fishes.

PREPARING FOR THE FISH

When the work of setting up the aquarium is complete it is a sound plan to leave it without fishes for as long a period as patience will allow—certainly not less than a week. The aquarium is given a chance to settle down in this way before the fishes

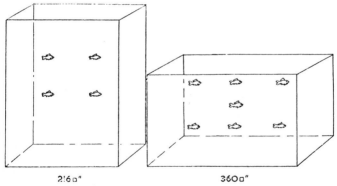

2'6□"   360□"

Fig. 4. Two tanks having the same gallon capacity but different top surface areas, showing the number of two-inch goldfish each will support without artificial aeration.

are introduced—and it is surprising the number of changes which take place during such a period of 'establishment'. It is several months before these changes are complete, but it will probably be noticed how in the early stages gas bubbles are released all over the tank, then these disappear and the water becomes increasingly clear day by day, until when the tank is really 'established' it has that crystal-clear appearance which is so difficult to explain.

Not infrequently during the course of this clearing process the water suddenly becomes quite opaque. This passes off after varying periods of time without any interference, and it is a mistake to clean out and start again when the cloudy water is seen at this stage, for it then recurs when the tank is set up again. This phenomenon is probably explained as a phase in the achievement of a stable population of the aquarium's microflora, and although, as remarked, it is sometimes a long phase, it is only temporary.

Next comes the question—how many fishes? At the beginning of this chapter it was said that oxygen availability was related to the surface area of the water, and that oxygen usage of fishes depends upon their size. These two factors can be linked to give an approximately true relationship and indication of an aquarium's fish capacity. The rule is that one inch of fish needs twenty-four square inches of water surface; in calculating the length of fish the tail (caudal fin) is left out for this purpose. Thus an aquarium with an aerial water surface of twenty-four inches by twelve inches, *i.e.* 288 square inches, can be used to keep twelve inches of fish (*e.g.*, six two-inch or four three-inch specimens). This is a safe rule to use, for it is calculated to leave an ample margin of safety for contingencies which might upset the aquarium's oxygen content.

There is an older rule for estimating capacity which allows an inch of fish to a gallon of water, but while this is reasonably safe to use when dealing with the conventional rectangular shallow aquaria, it will be realized that as it ignores the important matter of the extent of the surface area the rule becomes valueless if applied to water in deep vessels. It has, too, the disadvantage that the water volume in a furnished tank can never be calculated as surely as can surface area.

WATER CIRCULATION

It was said at the beginning of this chapter that one of the ways in which replacement of oxygen in the aquarium can be aided is by agitating the water. This creates a circulation in the aquarium, and an obvious way to achieve this is to arrange a small water pump to do the work. In practice, however, such an arrangement could only be justified if a large number of aquaria were kept, and even then circulation of water between tanks can be responsible for transferring disease or parasites from an infected tank to the others. The method usually employed with small collections of aquaria is to 'aerate' them with a stream of air bubbles from an aerator.

Artificial aeration of goldfish aquaria is not a strict necessity, but an aerator is a very useful aquarium accessory for the man with several tanks, and for the breeder. There are two kinds of aerators, both operated by electricity: mechanical pump types possessing driven pistons, and vibrator types having rubber diaphragms. The latter variety is the cheaper, but the air pump has the advantages of a much longer life and a greater output of air; it is also more silent in operation. By using an air reservoir into which air can be pumped by a hand pump a quite serviceable non-mechanical aerator may be made. The reservoir can be an old motor tyre inner tube or a stout metal can with valves from an inner tube soldered into it. By means of an adjustable clip on the outlet tube a flow of air lasting several hours will be supplied from the charged reservoir.

Rubber or plastic tubing leads the air from the aerator to the aquarium, where it is released as a fine mist of bubbles under the water through a porous stone diffuser. The stream of bubbles keeps the water in constant movement, and in fact this is a means of increasing the air-water surface area in an aquarium. Aeration alone will not permit the aquarist to keep more fishes in a tank than it is really meant to contain for long periods, but as an emergency measure for a short time it does enable some degree of overcrowding to be tolerated and also brings relief to a cold-water aquarium in which the water temperature has become excessively high (during hot, thundery weather for example).

One air-releasing stone is all that is needed for each twenty-four inch by twelve inch by fifteen inch aquarium. The flow of air should be adjusted to near to the minimum through the diffuser, for violent turbulence in the water caused by high rates of air flow will make the aquarium water assume a cloudy appearance; this arises from suspended fine particles of solids which never have the chance to settle under these conditions. Because the feeding habits of goldfish with some kinds of food commonly used encourage the formation of particle suspensions in the water, it is unfortunately true that even with moderate aeration goldfish aquaria are seldom perfectly clear. There is a method of obtaining a beneficial movement of water in the aquarium plus its aeration but without giving rise to cloudy tanks, however; this is the method of filtration.

AQUARIUM FILTRATION

To keep the water of a goldfish tank free from suspended food or other particles it needs to be filtered continuously, or at least for a prolonged period each day. Some form of pump is required to achieve this, and again the aerator is the cheapest and most readily available form for this purpose. The flow of air it yields can be utilized to 'lift' water out of the tank into the filter or may be employed to 'lift' it back into the tank after it has passed through a filtering medium. The principle used here is known as the 'air-lift', and which of the above two procedures is carried out depends upon the type of filter.

Some filters are made to fit within the aquarium; others (of larger capacity) stand outside it. In the first type, the air-lift tube, which is commonly made of celluloid and which has a narrower tube alongside it feeding a slow stream of air from an aerator into its lower end, carries a box for the filter medium at its upper end above the water surface. As each bubble forms within the tube and rises in it, a small amount of water is trapped between it and the preceding bubble; this water is carried to the top with the air and passes through the filter before dropping back into the tank. Water is delivered by a slow siphon into the exterior type of filter, and from this an air-lift tube returns it filtered to the aquarium.

Glass wool forms the best filtering medium for the finest particles, and it can be used alone or together with layers of sands of varying grain size to remove larger particles. Cotton wool can also be used, but it very soon forms an impermeable mat; glass wool is to be preferred. The layer is taken out and thrown away about once a fortnight and replaced with fresh. Carbon is also

sold for use in filters to remove dissolved materials from the
water by absorption, in contrast to the particle separation

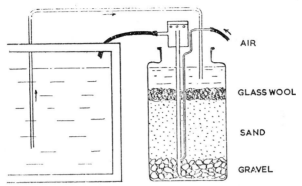

Fig. 5. The principle of the 'air-lift' used in an external
filter with an aerator to provide continuous filtration of aquarium water.

afforded by sand or glass wool. Apart from the fact that carbon
thereby robs the water plants of some of their supply of nourish-
ment it rapidly becomes saturated and requires replacing frequently if it is to continue functioning.

AQUARIUM MAINTENANCE
  Regular servicing of the aquarium is recommended to keep it
in good condition. A period should be set aside for this job every
week, and then it need not take up very much time. First remove
any algæ which may have formed a green layer over the inside
glass. This is done by scraping with a razor blade and rubbing
with a pad of newspaper. Then look over the water plants and remove dead leaves or any masses of thread algæ which may have
grown. Cut back plants which have become too long for the
depth of water and plant the cuttings in the sand. Lastly, siphon
out the accumulation of sediment from the sand surface. The
bulk of the detritus should collect near the front glass if the sand
is sloped so that it is less deep there, and this makes the siphoning a simple task.

A length of rubber tubing forms the siphon, and it is filled
with water by immersing it completely in the aquarium. One end
of the tube is pinched, and while the other end remains submerged it is taken out of the tank and held over a bucket. When
this end is freed water will begin to flow, and the siphoning
action continues as long as the outer end is lower than the end
within the tank. Move the tube in the aquarium over the sand

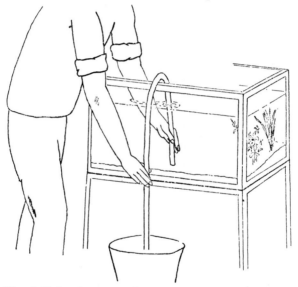

Fig. 6. Siphoning water from an aquarium. The tank
bottom can be cleaned in this way.

surface so that the sediment is sucked up with the outflowing
water. The removed water is thrown away and fresh water is
poured in to restore the original level. This partial change of
water is specially recommended for goldfish aquaria, and should
be undertaken every week or so even if it happens that there is no
need to use the siphon for sediment removal.

Sometimes a thin film or scum forms on the aquarium water
surface as a result of deposits of dust, etc., from the air. The best

way to remove this is to lay a sheet of clean newspaper on the surface, and then when this begins to be soaked with the water, to draw it off sideways. The film will stick to the paper and be removed with it. The white residue which forms round the water's edge during evaporation from aquaria filled from a hard water supply can be scraped off with a razor blade.

OTHER OCCUPANTS FOR THE GOLDFISH TANK

There are many kinds of fishes which will live peaceably in an aquarium with goldfish, but space limitations usually dictate that the tank be used for goldfish alone. A wise rule to observe scrupulously is never to add fish recently caught from natural rivers or ponds to an aquarium housing healthy fish. Parasites and diseases can be introduced in this way and will seriously affect the aquarium fish, since these will not have the immunity or tolerance of attack possessed by wild stock.

Bitterling, bleak, small carp, minnows, small golden orfe, rudd, tench and catfish are species which can form a community of fishes with goldfish in a large aquarium, if this is desired. Of these species, those which grow to a large size can be obtained as young fishes, and they may have to be moved to a pond if they reach large proportions.

Fig. 7. Two common water snails—*left*, the ramshorn snail (*Planorbis*); *right*, the fresh-water whelk (*Limnæa*).

Water snails are often included in aquaria, and there is no objection to having some of the varieties present if the tank is not used for breeding fish. Their presence is not essential to the well-being of the aquarium, and although they may clear some of the algæ which grows they will also eat water plants and may reproduce to such an extent that they become a nuisance. Goldfish eat newly hatched snails, and this can be used as an argument for including them, as well as the fact that they are amusing to watch in the tank. The ramshorn snail (*Planorbis*) is a relatively harmless species and there is an aquarium variety having a beautiful red colour. The warning given above concerning the danger of introducing wild fishes to aquaria applies also to water snails collected from natural waters; water snails are intermediate hosts to several parasites which in their adult stages live on fish.

CHAPTER 2

THE GOLDFISH POND

GOLDFISH are ideal fish for the garden pond or ornamental lily pool, not only because their colour renders them easily seen in the water but because they are not so active that their main requirement is a lot of swimming space. It is well, though, that their pond should be planned with some thought for the habits of the fish to live in it.

The surroundings of the site chosen for the pond will probably decide its external features—whether it is to be a sunken or a raised pond, or formal or informal in design. Informal ponds offer more difficulties for the builder by reason of their irregular shape; formal ponds, with their regular angles, straight lines and symmetry, are much easier to make. The formal pond would, however, appear obviously out of place in a garden not laid out in a formal manner.

Sunken ponds necessitate an excavation, but are preferable to raised ponds for fish-keeping in this country, since they are less readily affected by temperature variations. What might be called the half-raised pond overcomes this objection to the raised pond in some degree; this is made by digging out the pond shape to slightly more than half the finished depth and using the displaced earth to form banks around the pond's edges. These banks support and enclose the top part of the pond, and they can be made into an attractive surrounding rock garden.

POND SITE AND DESIGN

Unless little choice offers itself, sites for the pond which should be avoided are: under trees, close to fences bordering public paths, and parts of the garden which receive the full blaze of the summer afternoon sun. The site is best not too far away from a tap for filling purposes, and if there is a drain to receive the emptied water somewhere near, so much the better. Details for pond construction are given in an appendix to this booklet, but some important features of the design and the functions they will fulfil can be mentioned now.

Variation in depth of the pond needs to be arranged to suit the

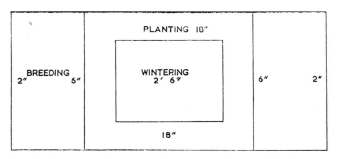

Fig. 8. Plan view of a pond with the varying depths of water provided by the stepped bottom marked on it.

breeding and wintering habits of the fish, and also to allow for water plant growth. For breeding, goldfish use shallow water —three inches to twelve inches deep; in winter it is advisable for the fish to have access to deeper water—about two feet six inches. Water plants require a depth of one to two feet. A plan which will allow these varying needs to be satisfied in the circumscribed regions of a small garden pond utilizes a 'stepped' pond bottom; this provides suitably disposed depths for all purposes.

On the steps or shallow 'shelves' reserved for the water plants is placed a three or four inch layer of clean, coarse sand as a rooting medium. On the bottom at the deepest part a little clean sand can be layered—one or two inches will suffice. No other bottom medium need be used, for plants such as water lilies which like to root in a rich compost can have this supplied within large pots or concrete troughs in which they are planted. When organically rich compost is used in this way it must have a three-inch layer of sand or shingle above it to stop goldfish stirring it up into the water and causing pollution.

POND PLANTING

The spring and early summer months make the best time of year for pond planting. For one reason, the plants are usually more easily obtained at this time, and when installed in a new pond in spring they have all the summer in which to become established. As noted in the last chapter, some of the water plants sold for ponds will be rooted; others are just cuttings which rapidly root themselves when planted in the sand.

You may know a stream or pond in which grow attractive, lush green plants and be tempted to use these for your pond. If wild plants are used they must be thoroughly washed and examined carefully all over for pests such as caterpillar-like aquatic insect larvæ and water beetles. The risk is also run of carrying microscopic parasites and infectious organisms along with the wild plants, and neither these organisms nor the eggs of various aquatic animals which may be present in the plants can easily be recognized or eliminated.

Plants in bunches tied with strong thread and clipped loosely with strips of lead to submerge them are planted in their place in the pond, after it has been nearly filled with water, with the aid of two long planting sticks. They are disposed all over the planting area with about one foot between each bunch of cuttings or single plant. The fully planted pond will have a more dense growth of plants than this, of course, the spacing recommended here being that allotted for a pond to be stocked for the first time.

Suitable water plants for pond use in water depths from twelve to twenty-four inches are: Canadian pond weed (*Elodea canadensis*), *Egeria densa*, hornwort (*Ceratophyllum demersum*), water milfoil (*Myriophyllum spicatum*), starwort (*Callitriche verna*), water crowfoot (*Ranunculus aquatilis*), water violet (*Hottonia palustris*), pondweed (*Potamogeton densus*),arrowhead (*Sagittaria natans*). On the water surface can be used tiny duckweeds (good food for goldfish, but floating plants which need strict supervision if they are not to over-run the pond) or crystalwort (*Riccia*), or one of the larger floating species such as frogbit or water soldier.

Water lilies are worthy of a few special notes. The large

surface leaves of pond lilies provide ideal shades from the sun for goldfish in the summer and help to prevent algæ growth, so that lilies would be desirable pond plants even if they did not form as well the beautiful blooms which make them specially favoured by the pond-keeper. It has already been indicated that lilies are not planted in the sand on the planting ledges but in special containers. These should be about a foot deep, and the rooted tubers of the lilies are placed in them with sieved, rich garden loam packed firmly around. A layer of coarse sand on top of the loam prevents dispersion of the soil in the water, and some large stones can be used on top of this to stop the tuber floating free when the container is placed under water.

The position for lilies in the pond should be one receiving the maximum amount of sun if they are to bloom well; another important consideration is to obtain the variety of lily most suited to the depth of water it is to inhabit. Water garden suppliers will recommend particular lily varieties to suit individual requirements. A recommended deep water (about two feet) species is the red-flowered *Nymphæa escarboucle*; *N. gladstoniana* has a white bloom and likes a similar depth of water, while *N. pygmæa helvola* is a yellow-bloomed species which will thrive in shallower water. The list to choose from is a long one, however, and if you can see a lily you fancy, growing and flowering in a park or botanical garden, then ascertain its name so that you can purchase the variety later on.

ESTABLISHING THE BALANCE

When the pond is planted it can with advantage be left without fish in it for a month. This period gives the plants time to form roots. During the first summer of the pond's existence the water is very likely to become cloudy and even green; this does not mean that there is something wrong with the pond, and it is a mistake to change the water at this stage. Any cloudiness will clear spontaneously in the course of several weeks, particularly as the water plants start to make good growth. It is disappointing when this water cloudiness is at its worst, but the clearing sometimes takes place very suddenly in a most impressive fashion, and this natural change should be patiently awaited.

The formula used for deciding fish capacity of the aquarium can also be used to give an estimate of the number of fishes the pond will maintain—one inch of fish to every twenty-four square inches of water surface. Do not stock to the maximum, however, so that room still exists for growth of the fish, and for breeding to occur; in hot, thundery weather, too, the recommended surface allowance for the fish may suddenly become inadequate, and fish in a fully stocked pool will suffer greater distress. Varieties of goldfish suitable for the pond, other than the common goldfish, are the comet, shubunkin and fantail; these will all live outdoors in a pond throughout the year. Other hardy gold-coloured fishes which are recommended as pond subjects and which will live together with goldfish are golden orfe, golden rudd, golden tench and Hi-goi or Japanese carp.

POND MAINTENANCE

Garden ponds require occasional attentions other than the visits made to them to admire or feed the fishes, particularly during the summer and autumn months. At these times goldfish have their greatest appetite, and they should be fed twice a day to make sure that they keep in good condition and form ample stores of fat to see them safely through winter's non-feeding months.

Under the influence of intense sunlight the plants, or some of them at least, may grow excessively and need trimming or removing; the tangled green masses of thread algæ ('blanket weed') may also run riot in the pond, and this pest needs to be removed periodically with a small rake. During very bright spells ponds in sunny areas can be shaded with sacking if the fish appear discomfited or if blanket weed is troublesome. If at any time in warm weather pond temperatures reach the seventies, or if the fish show signs of distress, cold water should be hosed gently into the pond.

In the autumn falling leaves are a nuisance in ponds situated close to trees. They should not be left in the water, for when they rot they are capable of causing pollution. A light screen of wire netting rested over the water surface at this time of the year will keep out the leaves. A useful implement for skimming leaves from the water surface can be made by screwing a square of perforated zinc to the end of a broomstick.

Small ponds should be given a thorough cleaning once every two or three years, and late October is the best time for this operation when it is necessary. Fishes can be netted after about half the water has been siphoned or drained away, and tanks or old baths of suitable size need to be collected together beforehand to house them while cleaning is in progress. Remove any sand from the pond bottom, washing it thoroughly to be ready for use again, and scrub the concrete sides before flushing the pond with clean water preparatory to returning the contents. Water plants can be given a good washing in fresh water, and any thickly choked with algæ are best discarded.

There is less to do around the pond during the winter. The fish lose appetite and water plants die back, but if the water becomes covered by ice at any time it is necessary to make holes in the sheet; if it is a thick layer it should not be broken·by a blow but by standing a hot kettle on its surface to melt it. Snow collecting on the unbroken part of the ice should be swept clear to admit light to the water. At the first signs of activity from the fish early in the spring their appetite should be tested with proffered earthworms. Dried foods are not used until full feeding is resumed.

POND PESTS

The number of kinds of strange aquatic creatures that can appear suddenly in a newly made garden pond, to the surprise of its owner, is a large one. Some may be installed with the water plants, but others reach the pond from the air; flies which breed near water soon arrive and lay their eggs on surface water leaves, where they hatch to produce various caterpillar-like animals. Water beetles from natural waters in the area may also invade garden ponds from the air; whilst it is quite possible for birds flying straight from the same source as the beetles to convey in the mud on their feet one or two more additions to the new pond's fauna.

Some invaders never get a chance to become established because they are eaten by the fishes, but the ones that the fish leave alone, for one reason or another, often develop into pond nuisances. They are not the parasites of fish but the water plant eaters, the fish egg and fish fry predators, and other types which do no particular damage but which by their weight of numbers alone cause the pond to appear unsightly. In addition, there are fish predators which are not themselves aquatic—cats, and birds such as the kingfisher and heron. Only preventive measures can be taken for these last pests; walls to the pond carried up at least four inches above the water level usually discourage angling cats, and a bright dangling object suspended over the water as a scare-crow will keep off all but the most persistent avian fishers.

Different sorts of nuisances are the amphibian invaders of spring time—the newts, frogs and toads. These visit the water in order to spawn about the month of March, and it is no easy matter to keep them out of ponds in country districts. Newts and their young will eat goldfish fry but not goldfish eggs; in addition, they rob the fish of any live foods present. Frogs add surface choking masses of spawn to the pond, and this must be thinned out so as to keep the major part of the water surface clear. The tadpoles which hatch do no harm and are in fact to be welcomed, for they are good pond scavengers and algæ eaters, and they provide excellent food for goldfish. Toad tadpoles are, however, not eaten by fish.

In their breeding zeal male frogs occasionally grip the larger

Fig. 9. Pond pests—dragonfly larva, *Dytiscus* water beetle and its larva (*right*). Approximately natural size.

goldfish and swim around with them, in the absence of a female partner of their own species; this results in the death of the fish if the grip prevents the movements of the gills. Fine mesh netting completely covering the pond area, placed in position about the beginning of March, may be used to exclude many of the amphibians, but if the frogs are allowed to use the pond make sure that there is some provision for them to return to land again after spawning. Frogs trapped in a pond will eventually die and their bodies will foul the water. Grass snakes are also liable to visit ponds in the country, and they are not above catching and swallowing goldfish of medium size. They may be attracted to the water initially by the presence of the frogs.

One of the most common pond predators is the large water beetle *Dytiscus*. The larva of this beetle, known as the water tiger, is a voracious feeder and will kill many young fish. All water beetles must rise to the surface periodically to obtain air, and patient vigil with a net at the pond edge, particularly after dark with the aid of a torch, is one way of catching them. The larva of the dragon fly is not unlike the water tiger superficially, and it too creates havoc among small fry in ponds. Both of these larvæ are large enough to be seen easily and captured with a net when they are in the upper parts of the pond, but unfortunately they spend long periods during the day hidden away on the pond bottom.

Several kinds of leeches are liable to find a home in the pond. Some of them do not molest fishes, but pond-owners usually view them as undesirables and try to eliminate them. They are recognized by their large, segmented worm-like bodies, wider at one end than the other when fully extended and having suckers on their under-surfaces, also by their looping movement over surfaces or undulating swimming motion through the water. In colour they can be brown, black or olive-green.

Planarians are flattened worm-like creatures somewhat smaller than leeches, black, brown or greyish-white, which move over surfaces with a gliding motion. Their vice in the pond is fish egg eating. Leeches and planarians can be caught and destroyed by lowering a perforated zinc cylinder containing raw meat as bait into the pond each evening and pulling it up some time after dark.

A tiny pest where newly hatched fry are concerned is the freshwater polyp *Hydra*. This is not easily seen in a pond unless water plants from the pond are removed and examined in a glass container. *Hydra* has a slender, tubular body with eight or so tentacles surrounding its mouth at one end of the tube; the other end fixes the animal to the plant leaf, rock or pond side. When disturbed the whole animal contracts from a length of about an inch to a barely discernible blob of jelly. The common water snail *Limnæa stagnalis* will eat *Hydra*, but apart from this method of control the only remedy in a badly infested small pond is to treat everything in it at pond cleaning time, when the fishes are removed, with household ammonia (one tablespoon to every five gallons of water). Infested plants are best destroyed, and the reminder can be given here that, like other pests, *Hydra* is

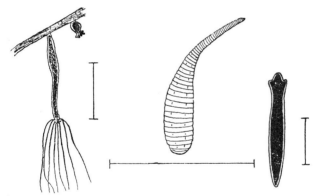

Fig. 10. Pond pests—*left,* extended and contracted specimens of *Hydra* seen on a leaf; *centre,* leech; *right,* planarian. Lines indicate approximate natural lengths.

most frequently introduced to ponds with plants collected from natural sources.

Blanket weed is the common plant life scourge of ponds in summer, for its green threads rapidly form unsightly tangled masses which choke the water plants. Although tedious, the only safe remedy is to rake out the mass regularly, with care not to trap small fish in it, and to pull out and destroy any plants thickly entangled with the growth.

WATER MOLLUSCS

Some of the objections to having water snails present with goldfish were given at the end of the last chapter, and the most serious charge which can be made against snails in the pond is that they will eat fish eggs. If breeding is not to be attempted in the pond then a few snails can be included, such as the ramshorn (*Planorbis*) or the viviparous snail (*Paludina*), for they undoubtedly act as scavengers and algæ eaters, though too much must not be expected from them in this capacity. Freshwater mussels can only do well in large ponds having a soft bottom medium in which they can move about. They are apt to die in small ponds and their decomposing bodies cause a lot of trouble.

CHAPTER 3

THE GOLDFISH

RED-COLOURED fishes are known from fourth-century records to have been present in rivers of southern China, amongst the greenish olive fish which are their wild ancestors and which are also found in these waters to this day. But it cannot be calculated at what period in the world's history the first of these coloured members of the carp family appeared. *Carassius auratus* is the scientific name of the goldfish, and its close relationship with the Crucian or Prussian carp *Carassius carassius* is indicated by anatomical similarities as well as by the fact that the two species will interbreed to give hybrid fish. Both these fishes probably shared a common ancestor, geographical separation being responsible for the dual development at a very early period.

CARP FAMILY

The family of fishes in which the genus *Carassius* is included is a large one termed the *Cyprinidae*. It also includes the true carps, in the genus *Cyprinus*, and these are distinguished from the goldfish and Crucian carp by the presence of barbels at the lips. Because of their importance as freshwater food fish, carp have been spread by man's agency far beyond their original southern Asiatic home. The wild goldfish is still sold for food in Chinese markets.

Since the Crucian carp and uncoloured or wild goldfish are the species most likely to be confused, their distinguishing features can be listed. The conspicuous row of scales bearing the pitted markings known as the lateral line on each side of the body is one feature used in descriptions of fishes; the Crucian carp has twenty-eight to thirty-five scales along this line, and it is found seven to nine scales below the dorsal spine or leading structure on the dorsal fin. Goldfish have twenty-five to thirty scales in the lateral line, and this row of scales is closer to the dorsal spine

—only four to six scales separate them. Deeper in the body than the goldfish, the Crucian carp also has a dorsal fin which is convex in outline owing to the gradually increasing length of the

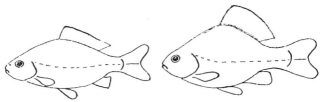

Fig. 11. Common goldfish (*left*) and Crucian carp
for comparison.

rays of this fin from the first to the fifth. The dorsal fin rays of the goldfish become shorter from before backwards, so that the fin's edge exhibits a straight or slightly depressed outline.

HISTORY OF THE GOLDFISH

Highly coloured descendants of the wild red-hued fishes had become popular pets in China by the thirteenth century, for evidence exists to show that they were being bred commercially at that time. The spread of the goldfish to ponds all over Asia took place through Japan, where it became established about the close of the fifteenth century. By 1700 the fish had reached Europe through the medium of ships trading in the East, but America received its first goldfish direct from Japan and not until well over a hundred years later. Throughout these centuries fancy varieties were being developed in large numbers; Mr. G. F. Hervey, to whom a lot of our knowledge of goldfish early history is due, has quoted an estimate of the number of varieties as 126, most of them known only to Eastern goldfish breeders.

Italy is the country today supplying Britain's pet market with goldfish, and large numbers of fish are flown to this country annually. Our summers do not encourage the development of goldfish breeding here on a commercial scale, and it seems likely that the unlimited sunshine and abundant supplies of pond live food available in Italy and similar countries are responsible for the rapid growth and early coloration of fish bred there.

EXTERNAL FEATURES

The typical external features by which all fishes are recognized as such and separated from other aquatic animals are the fins and scales. As will be seen from the next chapter, the fins of the fancy varieties of goldfish are often developed greatly in excess of the amount of finnage possessed by common goldfish and other species; the finnage of the common goldfish is, however, quite typical for fishes as a class in number, disposition, form and naming.

Fins have the function of controlling the movements of a fish more than initiating them. Movements of the body accomplished by contractions of the powerful muscles along the flanks of a fish propel it through the water. The tail, bearing the caudal fin, does of course assist considerably in this propulsion, but the other fins make smooth movements and changes of direction possible by their stabilizing, balancing and braking actions. Rotational tendencies induced by the body side to side and up and down movements are counteracted by the dorsal fin, situated on the back of the fish, and by the anal fin, which is on the underside of the fish just behind its vent.

The caudal, dorsal and anal fins are each single structures. The other fins are paired and may be regarded in an evolutionary sense as the beginnings of limbs. They are the pectorals, one each side of the body below and behind the gill covers, and the pelvics (sometimes called ventrals) situated close together on the body undersurface a little way forward from the vent. The rays seen in the fins are actually parts of the fish skeleton—short bony lengths socketed so that they are freely movable.

The scales covering the body are protective, overlapping hard plates bedded in the skin. They are transparent and are actually beneath the thin epidermal skin layer. On the body surface is a covering of mucus produced by glands in the skin; it, too, is protective, but it also serves to eliminate skin friction tending to interfere with underwater movements. Although some varieties of goldfish are termed scaleless, this is a misnomer. All goldfish have scales, but the characteristic appearance of the 'calico varieties' in which the scales are less conspicuous is due to the

PLATE I. Male Common Goldfish showing residual black pigmentation and also breeding tubercles on the gill cover.

PLATE II. Young Fantail Goldfish.

PLATE III. Veiltail Goldfish.

PLATE IV. Telescope-eyed Veiltail Goldfish.

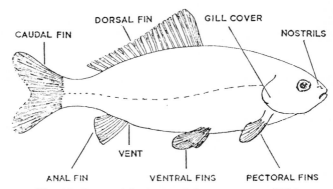

Fig. 12. External features of the common goldfish.

absence of a special layer of tissue normally occurring beneath fish scales which gives them a metallic appearance like the silvery backing to a mirror. The gill plates of the calico fish suffer the same defect, so that they have a 'soft' appearance and reveal the red colour of the gills beneath them.

At the beginning of the chapter differences between the numbers of scales were quoted for various members of the carp family, as characters serving to identify them. From youth to extreme age these numbers of scales on a fish remain the same unless lost by accident, and as growth occurs each scale increases in size at its periphery. Since growth is uneven, rapid phases of size increase alternating with quiescent periods when feeding is restricted, patterns of these phases in ring form develop on the scales; examination of the scale rings can enable an experienced observer to estimate the age of a fish.

Size of a goldfish is no reliable indication of its age, for size is influenced by the amount of food that has been available to the fish and by the conditions under which it has been kept. Growth is inhibited if the fish is kept in a small container, though if other conditions are satisfactory it will remain in good health. The maximum age to which goldfish live is about twenty-five years; the average age they attain is around ten years. Goldfish weighing two and a half pounds have been recorded in Prospect Park

Lake, U.S.A., and these must be very large fish when it is thought that goldfish eight inches in length weigh only a quarter of a pound! Greatest increase occurs in girth rather than in length with increasing age, and twelve to eighteen inches is about the maximum length commonly reached by goldfish kept in ponds. Fancy goldfish do not grow to anything like this extent.

SENSE ORGANS

Mention has already been made of the lateral line of goldfish. Each scale on this line on either side of the fish is pierced by a small pore, allowing contact between the surrounding water and sensitive endings of small nerves springing from a larger nerve whose course is marked by the pitted row. It is known that by means of these nerves the goldfish is sensitive to low frequency vibrations in the water, such as those set up by the approach of the fish to surrounding objects. The fish is also appraised of serious temperature differences within the water in which it swims by means of thermo-sensitive organs in its lateral line, and it is likely that this important body surface receptor has other safety functions as yet not elucidated.

The sense of smell is well developed in fishes, for vision under water is often limited by muddy surroundings and poor light penetration, so that the presence of food must be detected by odours arising from it rather than by visual contact. The nostrils of a goldfish are used solely for smelling—they have no connection with the mouth and play no part in respiration. Each nostril has two holes separated by a conspicuous flap of skin, and water currents are drawn into the foremost opening and expelled at the rear one; odoriferous molecules in the water are recognized by the special olfactory tissue lining the 'pit' into which the holes open.

Goldfish do not have an external ear, but there are primitive organs of hearing each side of the head (invisible from the surface), and these are sensitive to high frequency vibrations or sound waves in the water. Most noticeable external features about the eyes of a fish are the absence of eyelids and the very limited range of movement they can make. In some of the fancy goldfish the tissue surrounding the eyeball develops into a puffy mass elevating the eye from the head and producing the so-called telescope-eyed fish.

ACTIVITIES

Goldfish in aquaria show varying patterns of activity. Sometimes regular daily rhythms are developed during which periods of swimming about the tank are separated by intervals in which the fish remain almost motionless in the water. During these inactive periods it may be assumed that the goldfish are in the state most closely resembling that known to us as sleep, but that the resting times are not restricted to the hours of darkness has been shown by special apparatus used to record the activity of goldfish in aquaria over several months.

One activity which is always taking place is that of respiration, evidenced by the regular movements of the gill covers and mouth. By these movements a current of water is drawn over the gill membranes, and oxygen dissolved in the water is taken up by the blood which is richly supplied to these organs. Carbon dioxide formed within the body of the fish is carried in solution in the blood to the gills and there passes out into the water bathing them, so that there is a two-way passage of dissolved gases at this site. When many fishes are kept together in a small volume of water not only does the water become depleted of oxygen but the exhaled carbon dioxide also accumulates.

Unfortunately the rate at which carbon dioxide can pass from the aquarium to the air through the water surface is much slower than the rate at which oxygen can there be dissolved, and the presence of raised concentrations of carbon dioxide seriously interferes with the capacity of the blood of the fish to transport and utilise the vital oxygen. In this respect relatively high carbon dioxide concentrations in water may be more serious causes of respiratory distress in aquarium fish than lowered oxygen content of the water.

Growing water plants in a well-lighted tank absorb carbon dioxide from the water, but this activity does not occur during the hours of darkness or in poor lighting. Liberation of carbon dioxide from the aquarium is expedited by agitation of the water or by the air flow from an aerator, conditions which were noted in Chapter 1 as promoting the replenishment of water oxygen. Very high concentrations of carbon dioxide in the water cause goldfish to show symptoms of paralysis, but such symptoms are not normally seen in aquaria, where the signs of moderately raised carbon dioxide concentration causing oxygen lack in the fish, even when oxygen content is only slightly lowered, are swimming at the water surface and sucking in air by the mouth.

Another activity of interest, of which no external evidence is given by the goldfish, is the battle of its tissues to prevent them becoming water-logged. The cells and fluids of the fish are rich in salts, and the tendency of natural physical forces is always to cause the surrounding water to enter the fish and dilute these body fluids. Water entry is restricted to some extent by the impervious scales covering the body, but water is absorbed by the gills, and goldfish are continually swallowing water which is absorbed by their intestines. All this absorbed water is eliminated by the medium of the kidneys, copious quantities of a very dilute urine being continually produced by the goldfish to maintain a constant composition of its internal fluids. The vent of the goldfish, by which the urine is excreted, is an opening used as well for the passage of fæces and also for the extrusion of the sex cells at breeding time.

CHAPTER 4

FANCY GOLDFISH VARIETIES

GOLDFISHES are particularly prone to produce progeny showing various degrees of malformation, and it must have been discovered very early by the Chinese and Japanese that by selective breeding these monstrosities could be perpetuated. Most bizarre forms of the fish have been recorded in the literature from earliest times, but most of these are ignored by breeders today. The fancy varieties best known to British breeders are the comet, fantail, shubunkin, veiltail, moor, lionhead, oranda and celestial goldfish.

Of these the first three can be said to be the most hardy. They are the only ones it is safe to try and keep out of doors in a pond all the year round. Some of the others will live outside during the warmer months, but they all need to be given the protection of an aquarium in a warm situation during the winter. Each variety will be described, and its special requirements discussed, in this chapter, and where no specific directions for feeding or breeding are given it can be assumed that the general information given in other chapters applies to the variety.

COMET GOLDFISH

The comet is a comparative newcomer to the ranks of the fancy varieties, and it also has the distinction of having its origin away from the orient. It was developed in the U.S.A. around the year 1880. In this variety it is the finnage which provides the chief distinguishing feature from the common goldfish, particularly the tail (caudal fin). This is as long as the body or longer, distinctly forked, and is carried fully spread and not folded or drooping. The dorsal fin is not particularly large, but it shows a marked concavity and its rear part is free and pointed. Other fins are pointed and are in pairs, except for the anal fin, which is single. The body is elongated with smooth curves above and below. Like the common goldfish the comet is visibly scaled and the most desirable specimens are coloured a rich red.

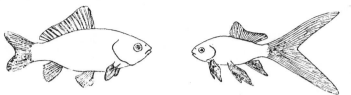

Fig. 13. *Left*, common goldfish; *right*, comet goldfish.

Being a rapid swimmer and an active fish, the comet, when fully grown, is an ideal fish for the pond. Young specimens may be kept in large aquaria but their movements are hampered. Fully grown comets commonly reach a length of seven inches. They are less readily obtainable than some other breeds, for very few breeders specialize in the comet, though why this should be it is difficult to say. One common fault with the variety is that the young fishes often take some time to lose their juvenile coloration before assuming the adult red. Comets breed readily in ponds.

FANTAIL GOLDFISH

First of the deep-bodied types listed here, the fantail is another hardy fancy variety for the pond and a fish which also does well in the aquarium. It first appeared some time during the sixteenth century, and both scaled and calico types are available. The calico fantail is a multi-coloured fish with blue, violet, red, brown, yellow and black markings, these colours intruding into the fins. Otherwise it resembles the scaled fantail, which is a deep, warm red in colour with uncoloured fins.

The fantail body is roughly the shape of an egg, definitely not spherical like some of the other fancy breeds. The dorsal fin is carried erect and in height should be about three-quarters the body depth. The pectoral, ventral and anal fins are all pairs, and the ventrals are large fins as deep as the body. The tail, which can be seen from above to be deeply cleft and divided so as to form four lobes, is carried in line with the body and without drooping or folding. Body length reaches three inches.

Mr. A. Boarder, an experienced breeder of this variety, recommends moderate heating for hatching the eggs and for rearing the fry up to three months of age; 70° F. is the temperature found most favourable. This means, of course, that eggs should be removed from the pond to sheltered hatching tanks. The adults do not need any artificial heating. Feeding is planned to encourage the full body of the good fantail, and oatmeal or cooked por-

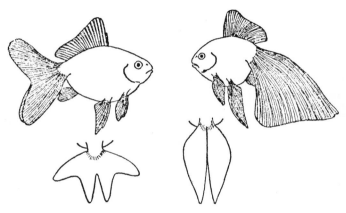

Fig. 14. *Left,* fantail goldfish; *right,* veiltail goldfish. The appearance of the tail of each fish from above is outlined below each drawing.

ridge given in addition to protein foods is excellent for this purpose.

SHUBUNKINS

It is not perfectly clear whether the shubunkin was known before 1900, but it is certainly since its introduction by the Japanese in that year that it has become established as an aquarium fish. Two varieties are recognized in Britain, known as the London shubunkin and the Bristol shubunkin. Both can be kept in ponds, though in the north, where severe winters are experienced, the Bristol type is better only wintered out in ponds of large size and having a deep part of about three feet.

London Shubunkin.—In body outline and finnage this fish resembles the common goldfish exactly. It is, however, a calico fish in its scaling, and the gill covers, too, should be transparent in appearance. In the variegated markings blue is the fancied predominant colour mingled with black, whilst violet, brown, red and yellow markings are also present.

Bristol Shubunkin.—This type has the streamlined body outline seen in the comet goldfish, and it too has a large tail. The tail in the Bristol shubunkin is broad and not pointed, however, and

Fig. 15. *Left,* Bristol shubunkin; *right,* London shubunkin.

neither is it flowing nor carried folded. The other finnage is well-developed and the tips of all fins are rounded. The calico scaling and coloration described for the London type is shared by the Bristol 'shu'.

Shubunkins reach a length of about seven inches, and when given good attention will breed in aquaria from the age of about twelve months. Large specimens need to be kept and bred in ponds or large aquaria, and it should be remembered that if youngsters are to reach full size they must be allowed plenty of space as well. The change of colour takes place early in shubunkins, so that culling of unpromising youngsters can begin a few weeks after hatching. For their first winter it is recommended that young shubunkins should be kept in aquaria and not in an outdoor pond.

VEILTAIL GOLDFISH

In the veiltail goldfish, first recorded some time during the sixteenth century, the tail is developed to an extent where its size greatly exceeds that of the body of the fish. As far as it is anatomically possible to do so, the body form approaches that of a sphere. With its leading edge rising nearly vertically from the back of the fish the dorsal fin is three-quarters the depth of the body. The pectoral, pelvic and anal fins are all paired and are long, broad and pointed; the pelvics are very conspicuous, being as long as the body is deep. The tail is completely divided along its mid-line, and is well spread so that the wide outer edges should form a horizontal line parallel to the body longitudinal axis.

Scaled veiltails with the same colour as the common goldfish, and calico veiltails having coloration like that of the calico fantail or shubunkin, are both recognized types of this variety. Body size of this fish is small, being perhaps three inches long in an eight-inch fish. The veiltail is not a hardy variety, but although adults cannot be kept in a pond throughout the year, they do not need special 'coddling' during winter. If kept in an aquarium situated so that the water temperature does not fall below 45° F. for long periods they will pass the winter without any trouble. Veiltails should not be offered food at such water temperatures, for, although the food may be eaten, digestion is then imperfect and intestinal troubles, with interference to normal balance and swimming, may result. Diet for these fishes should contain a good proportion of protein and not consist entirely of carbo-hydrate (starchy) foods.

Breeding cannot satisfactorily be attempted in an aquarium less than thirty-six inches by fifteen inches by fifteen inches. Carefully selected fishes are used for breeding because only from parent veiltails themselves originating from good strain will a useful proportion of young fishes with the desired characteristics be produced. Water temperatures should be in the region of 65° F. in the breeding aquarium, and the fry hatched and reared in water no colder than this. To rear five good veiltails from every hundred fry would be a creditable performance even from a good breeding strain—in most strains the yield of good fry is even lower.

TELESCOPE-EYED GOLDFISH

Telescope eyes is the name given to the protruding orbits seen in some of the fancy varieties. In these the eyes appear to be placed at the end of short puffy cylinders on the head of the fish. They occur in the fantail and veiltail goldfish (in both the scaled and the calico types) and also in the variety known as the moor. Goldfish with telescope eyes (the eyes are immovable, so are not really telescope-like) were recorded in China during the eighteenth century. Special attention must be given to the feeding of these fish, for their vision is poor and they may easily miss food added to their aquarium.

Moors.—The characteristics of the moors are their protuberant eyes and their uniform velvety-black coloration. They may have the body and finnage of a fantail (fantail moor), or the features of a veiltail (veiltail moor), but they are always scaled fishes and completely black. The eyes of the moors are uncoloured. Many fishes sold as moors lack the required black coloration and are bronze, or show areas with scales of burnished

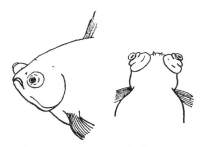

Fig. 16. Views of the head of a telescope-
eyed goldfish.

appearance. Even some black specimens may become bronze with increasing years.

Moors are relatively small fishes, and they will breed in a twenty-four inch by twelve inch by fifteen inch aquarium. Veiltail moors are the most difficult type to produce, but neither these nor the fantail moors can be safely exposed to the winter temperatures of ponds situated in regions having severe weather. Temperatures between 60° and 70° F. suit these fishes best.

LIONHEAD GOLDFISH AND THE ORANDA

Both of these rather rare varieties have heads which are covered with a conspicuous raspberry-like growth of soft skin. It has been suggested that these growths probably are the result of

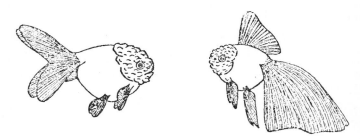

Fig. 17. *Left*, lionhead goldfish; *right*, the oranda.

a genetical defect in the strains which causes abnormal response of the tissue to the hormone testosterone released within the mature male fish. They are not present in young fishes, although females can also show well-developed 'hoods' or head growths. In body shape both lionhead and oranda resemble the veiltail, though only the latter fish has the same finnage as this variety. The lionhead lacks a dorsal fin, and its other fins, including the tail, resemble those of the fantail goldfish.

These varieties may be scaled or calico, having the colour of the common goldfish or that of the shubunkin respectively, in each of these types. Specimens which are white with splashes of red on them are commonly seen. The lionhead was the first of these hooded varieties to be produced in Japan in the nineteenth century, and the oranda was produced from it by crossing with a veiltail in 1840. Sub-tropical conditions are used in aquaria for these fishes, with temperatures in the range of 65° to 70° F., but they have been bred in outside ponds in south-western England and kept in the open throughout the year.

CELESTIAL GOLDFISH

The celestial goldfish may have originated in Korea, where it is said to have been an object of religious significance in temples there. It was introduced to us from China, however, and it is not a common fish in Britain today. In shape it resembles the fantail goldfish, but like the lionhead it lacks a dorsal fin. It has protuberant eyes set in the top of its head so that its field of vision is above the fish; these odd features give it a most peculiar appearance. In colour it is gold, pink or pearl-white with patches of red. This is another sub-tropical variety and one which requires a great deal of attention to keep it and breed it successfully.

STANDARDS FOR FANCY GOLDFISH

Standards for judging fancy goldfish at shows have been in existence since 1930, when the British Aquarists Association first introduced them. When this body became defunct these original standards were modified and are used today by the Bristol Aquarists' Society. Standards approved by the Federation of British Aquatic Societies were introduced in 1947, and are applied at most shows of fishes in Britain at the present time. A third, completely new approach to goldfish standards was made by the Goldfish Society of Great Britain in 1950, and brief details of these newer standards are given here for the sake of completeness.

Only four basic varieties of fancy goldfish are now recognized by the G.S.G.B. The standards for these were made after examination of a large number of quality fishes of the varieties dealt with in this chapter, and the Society claims that, unlike the old standards, their four basic varieties represent fishes which it is possible to breed selectively. The four varieties have been named: *singletail* (caudal fin terminating in a single, undivided fin); *twintail* (short caudal region with completely divided anal and caudal fins); *globe-eye* (large, bulging eyes); *bramblehead* (bramble-like growth on the head).

In addition, the G.S.G.B. has asked for the abolition of the terms 'scaled' and 'scaleless, calico or mottled'. It is claimed that the foregoing terms are inaccurate and misleading since all normal goldfish possess scales, and since the true variable factor which gives varieties their different surface appearance is the density of the layer of reflecting tissue beneath the scales. Three variations of this are described by the Society as (1) *metallic* (maximum amount of reflecting tissue—burnished metal appearance of the fish); (2) *nacreous* (intermediate amount of reflecting tissue—fish has partly or wholly the appearance of mother-of-pearl); (3) *matt* (little or no reflecting tissue—matt appearance of the fish). Each of the four basic varieties of fish recognized by the G.S.G.B.—singletail, twintail, globe-eye and bramblehead —may have an appearance placing it in any of the three groups denoting surface differences—metallic, nacreous and matt.

CHAPTER 5

GOLDFISH SELECTION, CARE AND FEEDING

WHEN buying goldfish, select your purchase with care. If you are buying direct from the breeder or from a reputable dealer you will be invited to pick out the fish you want from an aquarium, and under these circumstances it will be found more difficult to choose between the fish displayed, since they are all likely to be in good health and of good quality. There are, however, many dealers' establishments where overcrowded tanks are common, and in which are to be found fishes which should not be offered for sale in view of their short expectation of life.

SELECTION OF GOLDFISH

If you must buy from such a shop insist on pointing out the fish you want, for even in the tanks of thin, miserable half-starved and half-asphyxiated specimens may be seen some fishes (perhaps the most recent arrivals) which are obviously worth saving. A healthy goldfish is distinguished by:

1. *Finnage.*—Fins should be clear, free from kinks or bends, and carried erect. If they are perpetually folded up the fish is in poor shape. Split fins should not exclude a fish otherwise judged to be healthy because tears soon heal under good conditions; but fish with frayed and ragged finnage resembling battered Japanese fans have probably received similar treatment and are not worth having. The dorsal fin in particular reflects the health of the fish—it should appear stiff and fully extended.

2. *Body Outline.*—Here the body outline is being considered only as an indication of state of health—not in relation to the possible acceptance of the fish in terms of show standards. Goldfish whose lower body surface from pectoral to anal fins is arched upwards and those whose upper surface is badly humped have been poorly nourished and are risky to buy. They will also show, in all probability, hollows around the eyes. Fishes having

these symptoms in the early stages can be rescued by proper feeding in clean conditions, but it is necessary to judge from the next listed distinguishing feature whether or not the fish has deteriorated beyond recovery.

Fig. 18. Typical appearance of an unhealthy goldfish.

3. *Activity.*—Goldfish swimming in unusual positions or progressing clumsily with great shaking movements of the rear portion of their bodies should be discarded on sight. The fish that can hold station on even keel in mid-water with gentle fin movements and which is also capable of a sudden speedy dart away when startled is a healthy specimen.

4. *General Appearance.*—In the handling of fishes during transport to the dealers it is likely that some damage to the scales of the fish will occur, but missing scales soon regenerate. Be careful to distinguish between damaged or missing scales and the presence of surface parasites such as fish lice, however, and scan the body surface for signs of patches of fungus or blood-streaked regions. If when the fish is examined in the water from above, its gill covers seem to stick out noticeably beyond the smooth curve of the body, it should be regarded as a sick fish.

TRANSPORTING THE FISH

How the fish will be transported from the suppliers to the pond or aquarium will depend upon the distance involved. For journeys of short duration and for small goldfish that familiar part of the equipment of the 'tiddler' catcher—the jam-jar—is an ideal container. Fish cans made of tinned iron, with perforated lids, are used to carry large goldfish and for the transport of a group of fish over long distances. They should not be filled to more than half their depth with water. One disadvantage of these cans is that if they should be tipped all the water is lost; a special type of lid which admits air yet makes the can unspillable is sometimes used. This has a metal tube soldered through it extending from the lid's inner surface to a distance equal to half the can's depth, but the tube needs to be quite smooth to avoid damaging the fish should they be thrown against it during travel.

Transfer of the goldfish from the jar or can to their new abode is carried out by first floating the container in the water for a time, to equalize the temperatures of the two masses of water approximately, and then by tipping the container gently to allow the outside water to flow into it. The fish will swim out from the container as it is held on its side, and when introduced by this means they do not become scared or dash wildly about with the attendant risk of injury in strange surroundings.

To net fish when emptying tanks or ponds use hand nets on rectangular or triangular frames; for goldfish, nets with a coarse mesh may be employed, and this will not hinder movement of the net in the water so that fairly rapid sweeps can be made. All movements of the net must be smooth, and to avoid panicking the fish the netting procedure should not be too long protracted. If there is space to use two nets, the fish may all the sooner be guided into a position where one of the nets can trap it within its mouth against the side of the tank. Then, when the fish is seen to retreat into the depth of the net it is drawn to the surface and its movements are gently restrained by a light grip with one hand around the outside of the net all the time it is out of water.

When a fish from an outside source is to be introduced to established tanks or ponds where there are stocks of healthy fishes, a period of quarantine for the newcomer is recommended. It should be kept in a tank without other fishes, under observation for about a fortnight, and then, if at the end of this time it still appears quite healthy and has good appetite, it can be transferred to permanent quarters. This procedure can save a great deal of trouble and prevent losses of valuable fish if carried out routinely.

BASIC FOODSTUFFS

The main materials of the diet of animals including fishes can be considered under these headings—protein, carbohydrate, fats, vitamins and minerals. Protein is the material from which body tissue is built up, and so it is specially required by young growing goldfish. Live foods and meat offal are sources of protein. Carbohydrates are oxidized or 'burnt' within the fish to provide the energy for muscular work and all body functions; they can also be converted by the body into fats which may then be stored in the tissues, to be used during the winter hibernation period, for example. Plant materials are largely carbohydrate in content.

Minerals and vitamins are required in relatively small amounts, the quantities of the vitamins necessary to maintain health being particularly small. They are, however, dietary essentials; without them normal body functions are upset. Minerals such as calcium and phosphorus are needed for bone formation, and iron is needed to make the important blood pigment, hæmoglobin. The form in which minerals and vitamins are best provided is the tissue of other living organisms, and to ensure that all requirements are met the goldfish diet must include a number of different natural foods. This is the reason why variety of diet is considered to be so important for the well-being of goldfish.

GOLDFISH FEEDING

Fishes vary in the natural diets they select. Some are carnivorous, others are herbivorous. Others again, although favouring either the meaty diet solely or almost entirely the vegetable diet, are also not averse to trying a little of the alternative diet as well. The goldfish is such a species. It is predominantly a herbivorous fish, an eater of plant foods, but it also likes various small invertebrates to be on the menu too. Even if this were not known from direct observation of the feeding habits of goldfish it could be adduced from evidence presented by the anatomist and physiologist.

Examination of an adult goldfish reveals that its food tract (alimentary canal) is a coiled tube measuring nearly a foot in total length. The possession of a lengthy alimentary canal is a characteristic of animals feeding mainly or entirely on vegetable matter. Along the length of this tube food-splitting enzymes are released for the process of digestion. From the types of enzyme found in the goldfish intestine it is learnt that although the fish is well equipped to digest carbohydrate food, it is less well able to cope with large quantities of meaty (protein) food, and still less able to digest much fatty food.

In most animals the main site of digestion of meat is the acid medium formed within the stomach—a large dilated muscular sac which is also used to store a meal awaiting or undergoing digestion, and which is situated on the course of the food canal in its upper part. This organ is absent in the goldfish, but part of its upper intestine is slightly enlarged to form the 'intestinal bulb', and this is capable of being considerably distended as food is passed into it and so can be used as a small food store; the intestinal bulb of the goldfish lacks the acid and pepsin secretions which make the stomach the meat-digesting organ in other animals however. The only protein-splitting enzyme in the goldfish appears to be the one known as trypsin, and this is secreted along the whole length of the alimentary canal and not in any one special region.

The amount of food taken by goldfish and the frequency with which they require feeding are related to the water temperature. Appetite is greatest about 60° to 65° F.; below 50° F. the fish stop feeding. When appetite is at its best goldfish in ponds are feeding continuously on whatever they can find. In aquaria there is less scope for the fish to find acceptable food, and they are thus totally dependent upon their owner. In full summer, food can be given three times a day to goldfish in aquaria, and twice a day to fish in ponds. Early morning and evening are suitable times to give food, but the important point is to ensure that only enough is given at each feed to satisfy the immediate requirements of the fish.

A convenient rule to observe is to allow sufficient food for it to be cleared up entirely, without any being left over, within a period of about ten minutes. The danger of giving so much food that excess is left in the tank after each meal is that over the course of time this leads to water fouling; the uneaten food rots and causes the water to become cloudy with bacterial growth. If food is always given at the same corner of the aquarium the risk can be lessened to some extent by giving special attention to the sand in this region when the periodical siphoning is carried out. Free-growing algæ, which cause the water to become green and soupy, also thrive in water which has been contaminated with excess food.

Special care needs to be taken over feeding in late autumn as appetites begin to fade, particularly with the pond fish; the amount of food given then needs to be progressively reduced. As soon as it is seen that the fish are showing little interest in their food—readily recognizable behaviour if feeding is always done at the same time and at the same part of the pond each day—no more food should be added to the water. In early spring occurs another difficult period, when fish will show slight appetite on some days and no appetite on others. Again the aquarist must feed accordingly. To sum up, when appetites are good a little food to be given regularly is the rule to follow, and at other times feeding is to be dictated by the responses of the fish to food offered.

It has been said that variety of foods is essential, and the frequency of feeding has now been discussed. What remain to be considered are the various kinds of foods which can conveniently be provided by the average fish-keeper for his fish. Undoubtedly the dried foods sold ready for use in packets are the most convenient of all, and if selected carefully this type of food can form the main item of diet, but it should not be allowed to become the sole item.

GOLDFISH FOODS

Most of the well-advertised packeted fish foods sold today have carefully selected and blended ingredients forming balanced mixtures of the basic foodstuffs. They are also graded by particle size, and the coarse grade is the one required for adult goldfish. If the food contains very many powder-like particles it is a good idea to pass it through muslin, to separate the useful particles from the dust. Very fine particles added to an aquarium are not eaten; they accumulate on the bottom and decay. It is advisable to keep all forms of dried food in screw-top jars, for if they are kept in open cartons in the humid environs of aquaria they soon become mouldy and unpalatable to the fish.

Oatmeal or any of the breakfast cereals are other acceptable dried foods for goldfish, and the proprietary vitamin cereals such as 'C.V.B.' or 'Bemax' form valuable occasional supplements. Dried shrimp and dried water fleas are sold for fish-feeding, and the first of these can easily be prepared by the aquarist from shrimps obtained from the fishmonger. All these dried foods will be more readily eaten by the fish if just before using them in the aquarium they are softened by immersion in warm water.

The average household kitchen can provide a number of scraps which will add variety to the goldfish menu—crumb of (brown) bread, mashed potato, porridge residues, chopped raw beef, liver or heart, hard-boiled egg yolk, spinach, cauliflower, fish or meat paste, biscuit crumbs, etc. Freshly swatted house flies (but not flies from fly-papers or those killed with sprays) can be given to goldfish, and the garden will yield another source of tasty insect food.

Many goldfish breeders have found that the best food of all is the earthworm. It is not always easy to find the small worms which can be given whole to the fish, but the large ones can be chopped up with a razor blade into suitable-sized pieces or shredded with the ingenious metal plates sold specially for this purpose. It is worth keeping one corner of the garden manured and damp to encourage the worms, and then they should be available throughout the year.

A useful addition to the garden of the fish-keeper is a water butt or an old, large bowl or kitchen sink placed in a shady corner. Filled with water, such a container can provide many live foods, especially if some rotting leaves and a few water plants are added to it. Mosquito larvæ will appear in it during summer and so will blood worms, both of which can be collected with a small fine-meshed net for the fish. A few specimens of the freshwater louse (*Asellus*) or freshwater shrimp (*Gammarus*)—these will often be found when bunches of water cress are being prepared for the table—introduced into the garden live food container can lead to the establishment of a small colony for feeding purposes later on.

Water fleas (*Daphnia*) can be collected from natural ponds by sweeping a large net made of fine-meshed nylon to and fro in the water, but it is advisable to examine the 'catch' in a glass jar when it is taken home so that any undesirable water creatures such as leeches and water beetles can be picked out. Mud worms (*Tubifex*) are stocked by most aquarists' suppliers; these red worms should be kept in shallow water under a slowly dripping tap for at least twelve hours before adding them to the aquarium.

Another live food that can be cultured conveniently is the white worm, if a small quantity of the worms is purchased to commence the culture. A shallow wooden box is filled with moist, sieved garden loam, and the worms are added to this. The loam is kept in a moist state by covering the box with glass, and food for the worms in the form of mashed potato, bread and milk, or porridge is placed in small amounts on the surface of the loam from time to time. A piece of sacking should be used to cover the box to keep the culture dark, and it must be placed in a cellar or out-house where the temperature does not fall below 50° F. or rise above 65° F. Worms collect in the soil near their food, and if some of it is placed in a saucer resting over boiling water the worms will emerge and can be gathered with the aid of forceps.

HOLIDAY TIMES

Novices sometimes worry about the welfare of their goldfish when they are planning a holiday away from home. Fortunately, if the fish are in good condition they may safely be left without food for periods of up to four weeks without serious effects. In ponds the fish will carry on quite normally; in aquaria the water plants may suffer a little as the fish turn more to these for food, but it is wiser on the whole to leave the fish unattended in this way than to trust them to the care of someone inexperienced in fish-keeping. Nearly always too much food is added to the aquarium by the inexperienced, and serious pollution can result.

A suggested method of avoiding this risk is to leave small packets each containing just the right amount of food for a single feeding, with the date on which each one is to be added to the aquarium, for the guidance of the caretaker. Explain that although the amounts appear small they are in fact perfectly adequate, and then the well-meaning friend will be dissuaded from obtaining and adding additional food.

CHAPTER 6

BREEDING GOLDFISH

GOLDFISH breed readily when kept under the conditions the opening chapters of this book recommended. So it is no great achievement for the fish-keeper to claim as his own when his fishes spawn. If he can rear and bring close to maturity anything more than a small fraction of the large number of fry to hatch after a spawning, however, then he can indeed feel proud of his prowess.

GOLDFISH BREEDING SEASON

Fishes which have been fed well will be sexually mature in their second summer, but in illustration of the principle that fish development depends very much upon the treatment given it can be added that not all fishes in their second season are ready to breed. Just as size is no reliable indication of age, so is age not a true index of the maturity of a fish reared under artificial conditions.

Once a goldfish has reached maturity—*i.e.,* when it has developed functional organs essential for reproduction of its kind (testes in the males, ovaries in the females), it will breed many times in the course of the few months which represent the season for breeding, in each year until its death. Within the gonads, as the sexual organs both male and female are jointly called, inside the body of the fish are developed the reproductive cells or gametes—the male testis forms sperms, and eggs (ova) are formed in the female ovary. These proliferate most rapidly in the early part of the year in goldfish kept in the northern hemisphere, so that they are ready to be shed during the breeding months of late April to August (Britain). In the southern hemisphere, for example in Australia, goldfish develop 'ripe gametes' in July and August and breed during the period September to January.

From these facts it may be guessed that the two main environmental changes associated with spring—increasing light intensity and duration, and rising water temperature—are responsible for initiating sexual development in goldfish, and experiments with other fishes add weight to the likelihood of this. Minnows and sticklebacks in aquaria have been shown to develop mature sexual organs and breeding coloration out of the breeding season after the provision of raised water temperatures and long periods of artificial illumination. For fishes generally, increasing water temperatures are believed to form the chief means of stimulating sexual activity. Several factors probably act in combination to bring about an actual spawning, however, for although goldfish spawn more than once during a season, data on water temperature and weather conditions collected at spawning times do not supply formulæ by which other spawnings can be predicted with confidence.

During the spawning act eggs from the females and sperms from the males meet in the water outside the bodies of the fishes, and it is then that fertilization (penetration of each egg by a single sperm) takes place. As the breeding season progresses, fewer and fewer eggs are deposited by individual females at each spawning, and for this reason, and because greater time is thereby given for the development of fry under beneficial summer conditions, fish-breeders concentrate on the broods from the early season. If a female has not spawned by the end of the season she may still pass out eggs in the absence of a male fish, though these eggs will not develop, of course. Alternatively, the eggs may be retained in the female's body and there absorbed; occasionally this retention leads to the trouble known as 'spawn-binding', where the mass of eggs decomposes within the female and may cause her death.

SEXING GOLDFISH

The female goldfish body develops a rounded and slightly swollen form when she is ready for breeding, and this is the only distinguishing sexual feature of the female. The males, too, can normally only be distinguished during the spawning season, for then they usually develop small pale-coloured raised spots (breeding tubercles) on their gill covers and sometimes on the forward parts of their pectoral fins as well. It has been demonstrated by experiments that a natural chemical secretion (a hormone) from the active testis of a male fish is probably responsible for the development of the breeding tubercles; when immature males were treated with this hormone, called testosterone, the tubercles appeared on the gill covers in just under a fortnight. Some females also formed the tubercles when they were treated with testosterone. The curious 'hood' growth on the head region of the lionhead and similar varieties of fancy goldfish may be due to an over-production of the skin tissue responsible for forming the tubercles.

Where both sexes are together in a large aquarium or in a pond their breeding season behaviour may clinch the matter of identifying the sexes. The males will be seen to be actively chasing the females sometimes several days before spawning commences. Goldfish have no external sexual organs by which males and females can be distinguished, and neither are there secondary sexual characters of finnage or coloration in these animals. Out of the breeding season goldfish are extremely difficult to sex, and at any time of the year poorly nurtured fishes and specimens kept under bad conditions may fail to show the distinguishing features of sex outlined above. Although they are justifiably more expensive, sexed specimens are sometimes available from breeders. In a random group of goldfishes obtained to stock a pond or large aquarium it is practically certain that both males and females will be present.

CROSSING

Since all the varieties of goldfish have a common ancestral origin they are all capable of inter-breeding. If different varieties are allowed to cross freely with one another, as can happen in a pond stocked with more than one kind of goldfish, then eventually the characters which are typical of the pure variety will not be seen in the fry resulting from the crosses. They will be goldfish, but body shape and finnage will be pitifully mixed; pitifully because the creation of a variety of goldfish capable of reproducing its own shape and form to a high degree when mated with another of its kind is a task which costs the breeder much patience and many years of hard work. It is undoing this work and wasting the adult fishes to permit them to inter-breed and to raise the fry then produced.

The only safeguard against crossing is to separate the varieties or their males and females in different ponds or aquaria at breeding time. It should be emphasized here that 'breeding true' is a description only relatively precise for the goldfish. In strains of a single variety which have been kept for years, some fry not having the full characters of the parents are still produced from the hatchings season after season. One of the breeder's tasks is to examine the fry as soon as they are of suitable size (from about six weeks after hatching) for form and finnage to be judged, so that only those youngsters having the typical appearance of the variety can be picked out and kept; the rest are ruthlessly eliminated from his stock. In fact, the numerical yield of 'good' fishes raised to maturity from a single spawning of any one of the fancy varieties is disappointingly small.

Perhaps this is the most important fact to realise about goldfish breeding—that because of the very mixed ancestry of these fish and their infinite variability, the fish do not consistently breed true to type. The common goldfish and all the fancy varieties are 'sports', and the tendency is ever present for them to revert to the original wild ancestral form. Goldfish of any variety turned into a pond to breed indiscriminately would in the course of time give rise to fish which, but for the occasional individual every few generations, would show little trace of the red or golden coloration. The natural state would have been restored.

SELECTIVE BREEDING

The goldfish breeder overcomes reversionary tendencies by excluding from his stock fish which fail to develop proper coloration in good time, and, if he is developing a fancy goldfish variety, by eliminating, too, all fish which do not show the characters of body or finnage he is trying to encourage. This often involves scrapping the greatest proportion of the fry produced each breeding season, but only by such a procedure can a nucleus of fishes with some of the characteristics of a true-breeding strain be built up.

It is at once apparent that in attempting to form such a strain of goldfish it is desirable to start with parent fish showing to the greatest possible extent the features it is hoped to develop. To buy a mature pair of fish like this would be extremely costly, if indeed a breeder could be found willing to sell. It is worth noting well, however, that a pair of relatively inferior fish, bought from the stock of a breeder who is breeding on selective lines, is far more likely to have progeny with a good proportion of well-apportioned fish than is a pair selected from a heterogeneous collection of fish merely because they showed fortuitously a few desirable points.

What are the points to look for in the parent fish and in the selection of the fry? For any goldfish variety a long list of these can be made to give the picture of the perfect fish, and such lists are made in the creation of show standards. But it has already been said that the perfect or near-perfect parents to begin the strain may be impossible for the new breeder to obtain, so that for a start a few really important characters in the fish are concentrated upon. The three main features are colour, body shape and finnage. Thus, one parent may be chosen for its desirable colour and reasonably good finnage, and the other, although its colour is poor, because it has the typical body shape for the variety. Ideally it is also helpful to know something of the history of the two fish as well—what sort of fish their parents were and at what age they lost their juvenile coloration and assumed the adult colour, for example. It is hardly necessary to mention that stock used for founding a strain needs to be active, healthy and young.

Sometimes difficulties are encountered by the refusal of the chosen parents to mate. In most obstinate instances it may be necessary, after all the tricks of inducing a spawning mentioned later on have been tried, to use the hand-spawning technique as a last resource. From the fry of the first parents, some showing the combined good points of their mother and father can be picked out. Patience has to be exercized in waiting for colour changes, to see what their final appearance is, but if satisfactory they are given special feeding and attention to bring them to maturity ready for the next step in the breeding of the line.

This involves mating the selected progeny back to either the male or the female parent. The fry resulting from this are again sorted and the best kept. When mature these fish are mated with their grandparents, and at this stage sibling matings between brothers and sisters can also be tried to provide a new breeding line which is developed through subsequent generations in the same way. Each breeding season's spawnings are carefully planned and brought about between chosen fish, eliminating all the 'duds' and keeping the fishes closely inbred. Provided that the original stock was free from hereditary weaknesses this inbreeding does no harm at all.

From all this it will be seen that selective breeding is a lengthy business; several breeding seasons must pass before results begin to be seen in the form of an increasing number of young fishes having the strain's typical features appearing in each spawning. Another obvious requirement for the line breeder is possession of plenty of aquarium space. Without this insufficient numbers of fry can be reared to obtain full advantage of the technique.

BREEDING IN PONDS

Although goldfish will breed in the average size of pond made in gardens, there is one special feature the pond should have, to encourage a spawning. This is a small bay of very shallow water; it can easily be made when the pond is laid down, or added to an existing pond in the form of a shelf at one edge gently sloping all the way from a water depth of about nine inches to a little above the water surface. Alternatively, if special ponds for breeding are being built, these can be about four feet by six feet in area and made with bottoms sloping from the top edge at one end to a depth of eighteen inches or thereabouts at the other end. Most fishes enter the shallows of natural ponds when spawning, and in the excitement of this time they will often splash right out of the water on to the damp edge of the pond and back again with noisy flaps of their bodies.

At the commencement of the breeding season bunches of fine-leaved water plants are generously disposed in the shallow region of the breeding pond ready to receive the eggs. The plants need not be rooted in this position—it is better that they should be secured there with lengths of string; they can then be removed easily together with the adherent eggs. Suitable plants are milfoil (*Myriophyllum*), willow moss (*Fontinalis*), water crowfoot (*Ranunculus*) or hornwort (*Ceratophyllum*). Some breeders use bunches of raffia instead of water plants to receive the eggs, and in fact most submerged fibrous or feathery materials seem to be acceptable to the fish. Even the usually pestilential blanket weed growth can be used as a spawning receptor. If the bulk of the

Fig. 19. Bunches of water plants are anchored with string in the shallows of the pond at breeding time

eggs spawned is to be gathered, it is advisable to limit the water plants to the shallow area only. A thorough examination of the pond should be made early in the season to see that fish egg-eaters such as water snails and the several invertebrate pond pests are absent. Wire-netting screens can be made for the pond to keep out frogs and toads which are also likely to visit the water early in spring for their own breeding.

When the pond water temperature climbs to about 50° F. the fish will need to be fed regularly, and before the breeding period the best food to offer them is probably earthworms from the garden. Large worms should be cut up into suitable-sized pieces. The earliest sign of breeding intent to be seen will be the 'driving' of the females by the males, when temperatures in the pond reach the upper fifties and sixties (usually about May). Most spawnings begin soon after daybreak and they last several hours, until mid-morning, so that when vigorous chasing of the females into the plant mass in the shallows is witnessed the plants can be examined closely to see if they are bearing eggs. These are seen as pin-head-sized blobs of clear jelly, scattered singly all over the plants and stuck firmly to their leaves.

If the plants are well covered with eggs it is necessary to remove the bunches to the hatching ponds or tanks, for as spawning excitement abates the parents will commence eating them. Fresh bunches of water plants are then placed in position in the shallows ready for the next spawning. If it is only required to raise a few of the fry then the eggs can be left in the pond with the adult fish to hatch, of course; in a well-planted pond a number will escape being eaten and will grow to full size without special attention. The number hatching can be increased by shutting off the shallow part of the pond with netting, glass or boards to keep the other fishes out, if hatching tanks are not to be used.

BREEDING IN AQUARIA

Aquarium breeding of goldfish can be used by those without ponds who wish to try their hand at fish-breeding and rearing, and of course aquaria have to be employed for those non-hardy fancy varieties of goldfish which cannot be kept in ponds. Within limits aquarium breeding can take place outside the normal pond breeding season, but it is inadvisable to encourage winter breeding by raising aquarium water temperature, for the foods necessary for the fry are not in good supply until summer. Use an aquarium kept in a well-lighted situation and one not less than twenty-four inches by twelve inches by fifteen inches in size. Larger aquaria are necessary for some varieties such as the veil-tail goldfish.

The breeding aquarium should have fresh, clear water and be planted thickly with water plants, but it is not necessary to have sand on the base. If sand is dispensed with the plants are kept submerged by tying the bunches to stones or by wrapping the ends of the bunches loosely with strips of lead or lead wire. A pane of glass which will fit vertically across the tank in the middle is useful and can be placed in position so that the male fish is on one side and the female on the other, during April. The fish must be mature, of course, and the female should show signs of being ready to breed in her bulging sides. Regular and ample feeding is instituted for several weeks, and then, in a period of sunny weather in May (if the sunshine reaches the aquarium, that is) remove the glass partition after dark one evening and reduce the water depth to about six inches. Water temperature should be about 65° F.

Spawning usually follows on the next morning, but if it does not, the fish are left together for a few days, and then, if spawning has still not occurred, they are separated by the glass partition for another week and the procedure is repeated. Spawning takes the same pattern in the aquarium as in the pond, the female being driven into the water plants by the male and bumped and prodded until her eggs are laid. There is a greater risk that eggs will be eaten as spawning drive diminishes in the close confines of an aquarium, so watch should be kept and the parent fishes removed when egg-eating is seen. The eggs are left to hatch in the aquarium and are cared for in the same way as described for the hatching tanks used in conjunction with the pond later on.

Occasionally the fish selected as parents refuse to spawn together. If they are healthy and, as far as can be judged, in the right condition for breeding, one or two dodges can be tried to induce them to spawn. Removing some of the water from the breeding aquarium and replacing it with fresh at a temperature five degrees lower can be tried. In the pond, fresh water can be hosed in to give the same effect. This should be done late one evening before the fishes are brought together, by the removal of the partition in the aquarium. An alternative expedient is to take up some of the water into a garden syringe and repeatedly discharge it back into the tank with some force so that air bubbles are carried into the water with the jets. A fountain may be run for a time in the pond or an aerator used in the aquarium to similar effect. These devices may not produce the required result the first time they are used, but it is wise to persevere with them at intervals, for spawning may follow at any time.

ARTIFICIAL SPAWNINGS

Artificial spawning methods are used and have been used for many years in commercial fish hatcheries all over the world for the propagation of economically important fishes such as trout. From the widespread use of this practice in such spheres it may be guessed that artificial spawning has many advantages to offer the serious fish-breeder. It has been applied to goldfish only in recent years, and credit for this development must go to two British aquarists—Mr. A. Boarder and Mr. C. E. C. Cole. The line breeder of goldfish and the student of heredity in these fish are the ones to whom artificial spawning is of greatest application, but the procedure is not specially difficult and can be used successfully by any experienced fish-keeper who cares to experiment with it.

Eggs and milt from mature fishes are collected and brought together for fertilization to occur under the control of the aquarist. The process of obtaining the gametes in their secreted medium is known as 'stripping' and does not harm the donor fishes if performed correctly.

1. The selected parent fishes are carefully netted in the breeding season and examined to ensure that they are 'ripe'—*i.e.,* ready for spawning. Adult fishes taken in early June (if they have not spawned naturally) will be seen on examination to have distended vents; sometimes reddening of the vent is also noticeable. Such fishes will readily provide gametes for the artificial spawning. They can, if desired, be treated to destroy any surface parasites on them by placing them in solutions of sea salt (two tablespoons to the gallon) for five minutes before stripping. Ripe fishes must be netted gently and not allowed to thrash about in the net, for violent movements will cause eggs and milt to be extruded prematurely.

2. As a container for the gametes a flat-bottomed shallow glass or earthenware pan such as a photographic dish is used. A refinement suggested by Mr. C. E. C. Cole is to place a sheet of glass ruled with large regular squares in the bottom of the dish; by this means the eggs are easily handled and counted. Usual hatchery procedure is to have the dish quite dry to receive eggs and milt, but the eggs of the goldfish are strongly adhesive and it aids even dispersion of them over the dish to use enough clean water to cover its bottom.

3. Stripping must be performed speedily, confidently and gently. Thoroughly wet the hands and with the left hand pick up the female goldfish. Cup the hand over her back holding her

comfortably yet restraining movements, and turn the hand so that she lies vent uppermost with this orifice pointing away from you and positioned over the dish. Then with two finger tips of the right hand stroke the sides of her belly with gentle pressure towards the vent. If the female is ripe, eggs will cascade out and can be distributed evenly in the dish by moving the fish to and fro over it, and by slightly rocking the dish occasionally. Next the male fish is caught and held over the dish in the same way; his milt is extruded into it by stroking the belly surface of the fish with gentle pressure towards the vent, when milt appears in a milky stream. In these procedures squeezing is *not* the technique to apply, and both fishes should be stripped within a few minutes.

4. With the milt and eggs in the dish, fertilization soon occurs

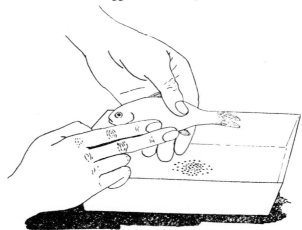

Fig. 20. 'Stripping' a female goldfish to obtain eggs

and dispersion is aided by tilting the dish backwards and forwards for several minutes. It is set aside for a quarter of an hour (this period covers the motile life of the sperms in the milt) and then the fertilized eggs, firmly adherent to the dish or glass plate, are washed with clean water flooded into the dish several times. From this stage onwards hatching and raising the fry follows the procedure outlined in the next section. Hatching can be allowed to take place in the dish if it is kept covered with glass in a suitable situation, or the glass plate can be transferred to shallow water in the rearing tank. With this method any white, infertile eggs can be readily seen and picked out with forceps.

5. The stripped male and female goldfish are returned to their aquaria as soon as they are finished with. Natural spawning of eggs remaining in the female often follows shortly afterwards. Nutritious food such as chopped earthworm should be given to settle the fish as soon as possible after stripping.

Advantages of artificial spawnings are:

(a) Spawnings can be timed to suit the aquarist. Pond spawnings often occur at inconvenient times for the owner wishing to save all the eggs.

(b) Eggs are obtained under clean conditions, uncontaminated by mud or plant debris and away from harmful pests such as snails.

(c) Greater numbers of fertile eggs are obtained; natural spawning during the chase is most wasteful of eggs and milt. This consideration is more important for the breeder wishing to have the maximum number of fry for observation.

(d) Scale or fin damage which sometimes occurs during energetic pond chasing is obviated by stripping prize goldfish also used for showing.

(e) Parent fish can be selected for desirable qualities and a brood is ensured even when a pair obstinately refuses to mate under aquarium or pond conditions.

Well over two thousand eggs may be obtained from a single female by the stripping method, and the aquarist needs ample facilities of space and for feeding if he is to cope with all the resultant fry. This, however, is a problem always with the fishkeeper, and the necessity of acknowledging limitations when dealing with fry is stressed in the following section.

HATCHING THE EGGS

Apart from the desirability of removing the eggs from the

PLATE V. Bristol Shubunkin.

PLATE VI. Male London Shubunkin showing breeding tubercles on the gill cover.

PLATE VII. Moor variety of Goldfish.

PLATE VIII. Celestial Goldfish.

PLATE IX. Lionhead Goldfish.

PLATE X. An unusual goldfish variety — the 'Bubble-eye.'

spawning quarters because the parents may eat them or the hatching fry, it is also a good move to make in order that the fry can be given special attention that cannot be given when they are in a pond. Feeding is easier, the baby fish can be examined more readily, and pests are less likely to appear in the hatching tanks. There is no harm to the eggs in taking them out of the water whilst they are attached to the water plants, and, in fact, if kept damp they can even be sent through the post in this way!

Hatching tanks need not be the conventional glass aquaria. Large-scale breeders use tanks of concrete, and an extremely cheap hatching tank is made by floating over the interior of an old metal water cistern with a mixture of equal parts of cement and sand in water. Two coats of this surfacing are given, time being allowed for the first to dry before the second is applied. Any pipe-holes in the tank can easily be blocked by wood bungs before the cement wash is given. When the tank interior is coated it must be filled with water, emptied and scrubbed and then re-filled and emptied several more times to wash out all excess of lime from the cement before it can be used for fishes.

Keep the hatching tanks where they will receive sunlight during the day and yet not be exposed to any late night frosts. An unheated greenhouse makes an ideal situation for them. Water from the pond or mains water which has been standing for a day or so is used to fill the tanks to a depth of about a foot. No sand is needed in the tanks. The water plants with the eggs are dropped into them and there left to hatch. Water temperature is best kept in the region of 70° F., and if a cold spell develops a low wattage aquarium immersion heater can be used to maintain the temperature, or else a paraffin heater can be kept burning near the tanks. At the recommended temperature the eggs will take about four days to hatch out.

One or two days after spawning some of the eggs may be seen to have turned white, or even 'fluffy', in the tanks. These are infertile eggs or ones that have failed to develop for some reason. At three days it should be possible to see occasional flicks of the fry in the developing eggs. When they first hatch, the fry are difficult to recognize; they do not move about very much and appear as tiny dark slivers clinging to the plants. They hatch with sacs filled with yolk attached to their undersurface, and this food is utilized by the young fish for the first forty-eight hours of their life. The hatching period is determined almost solely by water temperature, and is speeded up by warmth or delayed by cold. At about 60° F. the eggs may take just over a week to hatch. It is important to keep the surface of the water in hatching tanks perfectly free from dust and scum, for newly hatched goldfish fry need ready access to the atmosphere in order to fill their air bladders. For the same reason the water in the tanks is kept shallow.

As soon as spring weather appears and before spawnings begin it is a good plan to place in the open a tank filled with water for this to become green with algæ. Under the influence of sunlight this growth will readily take place, and by the time the first fry have hatched there will be on hand a tank filled with their first food.

FRY FEEDING AND REARING

Two days after hatching (about a week after the eggs were laid) fry feeding should begin. About twice a day a large jug filled with the green water is tipped into each hatching tank and a similar quantity is taken out and returned to the 'green tank'. This method of feeding will suffice for up to the tenth day of the fry's life, and they will be feeding continuously during daylight hours through this period. They will grow more quickly if artificial lighting is also supplied at night, though this is not really necessary for tanks kept outside. Indoor aquaria should have some artificial lighting (from above) or the fry will progress too slowly. In the event of there being no green water available, food suspensions can be prepared for the fry.

One food which is easily obtainable and which is no trouble to prepare is egg-yolk, and the nutritional value of this is very high. It is prepared for use by vigorously stirring some of the hard-boiled yolk into a cup of water so as to form a heavy suspension of small particles of yolk. This suspension can then be added to the fry aquarium at intervals. Once the particles settle out from suspension in the aquarium water the fry make no use of them as food, so that it is necessary to avoid adding a large amount of the egg-yolk at a single feeding, and it is helpful to have a moderately good supply of air from an aerator to agitate the water and prevent the particles settling. If too much of this food is given and if uneaten particles *are* allowed to accumulate on the aquarium base the losses in fry will be heavy, for in the decomposition of egg extremely poisonous sulphur-containing compounds are released into the water.

Other foods normally given to adult fishes can be fed to fry by the employment of this fine suspension method. Pulped earthworms stirred into water make a nutritious and much-liked 'broth' for fry, and liver, heart, kidney or even fish paste can be used in the same way. For a large aquarium containing fry a jar of any of these food suspensions can be actually immersed in the tank and allowed to stand on the bottom, mouth upwards; the fry soon learn to congregate in and around it and rapidly clear its contents.

An older method of feeding fry is to make cultures of Infusoria. This is the name given to a large variety of microscopic and semi-microscopic primitive forms of life which develop in water containing decaying vegetable matter. With green water (which is also likely to contain Infusoria), these organisms are the food taken by fry under natural conditions. Cultures are made by filling a two-pound jam-jar with aquarium water in which is stirred a pinch of pond mud or earth from a damp corner of the garden. Added to the jar is a lettuce leaf, an old banana skin, a piece of soft potato or a spoonful of milk, and then the mixture is stored in a warm place.

After a day another jar is started in the same way and a little of the contents of the first jar is also added to it. Fresh jars are started daily so that there is a succession to hand. The first will be ready for use after about three days, when the fluid in it should be strained through silk to trap the Infusorians. The silk is shaken in a jar of fresh water and then this clean Infusoria-containing water can be added to the fry tank. Tiny moving specks should be visible to magnifying glass examination of a drop of the culture, which is of no use unless these are seen. Duckweed (*Lemna minor*) can be used with advantage as a surface plant in ponds containing young fry because its presence encourages the production of Infusoria.

Micro worms are also cultured for use in fry feeding during the first weeks after hatching. Dealers supply these worms, which are bred in small glass pots containing a paste of boiled oatmeal. Wetted matchsticks are stuck into this medium, and the worms climb on to these and may be rinsed from them into the fry tanks. The culture jars of medium need to be renewed from time to time, a little of the old medium being used to carry a fresh stock of worms over to the new jar, and most rapid reproduction occurs when the jars are kept at about 70° F.

At four weeks of age the fry should be large enough to take chopped *Tubifex* worms and the larger particles from shredded earthworm suspensions. Water fleas (*Daphnia*) can also be given if these are obtainable. The frequency of feeding will be dictated by the appetites of the fry and by the time their keeper can spare to attend to these. It is no use trying to add a lot of food only once a day, for serious risk of water fouling is run in this way. Giving sufficient amounts for the fry to clear up completely within an hour (and only experience will teach what a tank of fry can consume) is the proper method. Depending on the water temperature and duration of lighting, three or four such feeds every twenty-four hours are likely to be the minimum.

Regular partial changes of the water in the tanks should be continued and a moderate trickle of air from an aerator diffuser stone will also be beneficial. The fry will have grown to a size at which overcrowding becomes a serious problem, so that they need to be thinned out into additional tanks. Six fish to every square foot of water surface in the rearing tanks is a safe allowance for maintenance of health and growth.

Some of the fry will be found to grow much more quickly than others. These larger ones should be kept together or they will rob the others of food and may even become big enough to make a meal of their brethren. Misshapen fry should be discernible easily at about a month, and these can be scrapped to give more space and food for the others. If the fishes are examined in a glass tank periodically the runts and malformed ones can be most easily picked out. An average length for the young fishes at this age is one inch, if they have received sufficient food and good attention. From this stage onwards feeding is much less of a problem and they can be given the same diet as adult goldfish.

The young fish are bronze in colour, and if they are from a good strain they should begin to change to golden when they are about two inches long. The calico types develop their colours earlier than the 'scaled' varieties. In most varieties the colour change should have started by six months after hatching and be complete in one year. Sunshine and moderately warm water temperatures are needed to develop the change, and apart from providing these conditions wherever possible there is nothing that can be done to hasten the process.

Young fishes of the hardy varieties which have reached a length of two inches in the body at the end of the summer (only those from the earliest spawnings will have done so, of course) are permitted to winter in the pond. Others must be kept in the aquarium until the following spring. Any artificial heating which has been used should have been discontinued well before the autumn so that the fish are prepared for the change of season.

CHAPTER 7

HEALTH OF THE GOLDFISH

THIS chapter largely forms a review of what may happen if the proper procedure of fish-keeping is not carried out in all its stages, for ill-health in goldfish is almost always the result of improper living conditions. The emphasis must always be on prevention, because it is unfortunately true that results of attempts to cure deviations from normal health in fish are frequently abortive.

Some reported methods of treatment have obviously originated from mistaken notions of the actions of drugs used in the treatment of human ailments which might appear to show symptoms identifiable with those of the fish disease. Only remedies which are thought to be the best available as far as present scanty knowledge of fish pathology indicates will here be included, although it is acknowledged that there is considerable room for improvements to be made. Common goldfish are quite hardy, and righting the faults in the environment is commonly enough to restore health to an ailing fish, so that it is undesirable to hasten to use chemical treatment unless that treatment is essential for the establishment of good living conditions. Fancy goldfish varieties are much less tolerant of bad conditions and careless feeding, it should be noted, and young goldfish fry are impossible to treat if they become ill.

Keeping goldfish in too closely confined quarters and giving inadequate feeding are perhaps the two most common causes of illness. Not only does overcrowding throw a strain on all the normal functions, for fish kept under these circumstances are always in a state near asphyxiation, but parasites are then given greater opportunity for transmission from fish to fish, and the consequences of their presence are always more serious for weakened fish. Wild fishes nearly always have internal or external parasites which they tolerate all their lives when under natural conditions; crowded together in an aquarium they begin to show the worst results of the parasitism.

Symptoms of ill-health in goldfish were listed in the notes on selection of fish in Chapter 5. Earliest signs are loss of appetite, sluggish swimming movements and a folded dorsal fin.. The ailing fish usually spends a lot of time at the water surface mouthing air, and does not dart away with normal vigour when disturbed. If a single fish shows these signs it should be kept under observation for any additional symptoms which might identify its complaint. When all the fish in an aquarium or pond show the same behaviour the episode must be viewed more seriously, and the conditions of their surroundings need to be checked over.

First-aid steps to be taken for the ailing fish include removing it from any possibility of overcrowding to shallow water (three to four inches deep), with artificial aeration if this can be provided. The water temperature should be kept in the region of 60° F., and while the fish is under observation or being given any specific treatment it should only be offered live foods (chopped earthworms are a recommended sick diet). Using water in which sea salt has been dissolved in the concentration of two tablespoons to the gallon, frequently has a tonic effect on the fish, and the solution should be changed for fresh daily.

COMMON COMPLAINTS

Fin congestion and fin rot are apparently related conditions occurring in goldfish. In the early stages blood streaks are seen in the tail fin and later in the other fins. Tissue between the fin rays gradually disappears so that the fins appear ragged and frayed—an appearance quite different from that given when accidental splits or tears have been caused. All the steps recommended above, including the salt bath, should be taken, and with fancy goldfish varieties the water temperature can be raised to about 70° F. with advantage. Poor living conditions and dietary deficiencies promote this complaint, and these factors obviously need to be rectified quickly. As the fish recovers, the fins start to mend and should be healed within a month.

Loss of balance occurs as a symptom of several goldfish disorders. The fish may swim on its side, head downwards, or it may be quite unable to rise from the bottom of the tank. In the round-bodied fancy varieties of goldfish this behaviour may be related to deficient development of the air bladder of the fish, and in all goldfish intestinal disturbances can cause the symptoms, possibly as a secondary result of interference with air bladder function. Where development is at fault no remedy can be applied, of course. If the diet has consisted almost entirely of dry food, then constipation can be suspected as a cause of the trouble; similar circumstances can arise if the fish has been suddenly chilled, since this halts digestion of food already taken; inflammatory conditions of the intestine arising from unknown causes may also be responsible. Shallow water, warmth and a live food and vegetable diet will accelerate recovery.

Fungus is the name given to the greyish or white tuft-like growth that occurs on pond goldfish. The fungus responsible *(Saprolegnia)* is nearly always present in natural waters in spore form, and it is specially likely to appear on a fish which has received a body or fin injury. Less easy to explain is the appearance of the growth on goldfish in spring and early summer when the fish otherwise look quite well. Sometimes the infestation is heavy, the fish trailing long fungal streamers, and it is almost as though some skin protective mechanism is lost during the winter rest period and takes time to be regenerated.

However, if the fish is feeding well and has no other complaint, fungus is not serious; this treatment is an old and reliable one: transfer the fish to a solution of sea salt, making this one ounce/gallon for the first day; second day, change to one and a half ounces/gallon; third day, change to two ounces/gallon; fourth day, change to two and a half ounces/gallon. Keep the fish in this last solution until the fungus starts to disappear, and then reverse the sequence of salt concentrations day by day and return the fish to fresh water. If injuries were responsible for the fungal attack try to find out how these were caused.

Injuries and wounds in goldfish mostly heal spontaneously if

fungus does not infect them, so when a fresh injury is seen the
fish should be netted, and while it is held out of water in the net
the raw place is dabbed with cotton wool soaked in surgical
iodine and then smeared over with vaseline. Split and torn fins
also mend spontaneously, and so do broken fin rays; regenera-
tion of lost or damaged rays does not occur in water below 60°
F., however, so it is only during summer months that pond goldfish mend their scars. The presence of some predatory animal at
the pond-side may be suspect if injuries frequently occur and if
fish disappear.

Distended bodies of goldfish accompanied by scale protrusion
above the normal surface may be identified as the complaint
called 'fish dropsy', but if the fish is a female and the symptoms
occur during late summer the condition may be spawn-binding.
German fishery research experts believe dropsy to be due to a
bacterium, others say that a virus is responsible; whatever the
cause the complaint is incurable at the present time, although the
salt bath treatment recommended for fungus may bring relief of
symptoms for a while. Spawn-binding arises when eggs are not
extruded, and when their decay within the fish occurs instead of
their being normally absorbed. 'Stripping' the fish in the way described in the last chapter may result in the expulsion of the
mass, but it also is helpful to keep the fish in warm water for a
time.

Eye complaints, usually manifested by an opacity of the eye
surface or of the pupil of one or both eyes, are incurable in goldfish, and blindness usually follows the onset of the eye signs.
Blindness in one eye does not incapacitate a goldfish very much,
but a totally blind fish should be destroyed. One form of blindness is caused by the penetration of the eyes by a parasitic larval
worm (*Diplostomum*), which also spends stages of its life cycle in
water snails and parasitizes aquatic birds in its adult worm stage.

Raised lumps—**tumours**—occurring on the body of a goldfish
are incurable and result in the death of the fish in time.

Wasting may occur in an old goldfish, making it appear hump-backed and causing it to lose its normal body outline generally. This can be due to senility, but wasting also occurs in fish tuberculosis (not contagious to humans) and of course when the fish has been kept without food or prevented from feeding for very long periods.

Coloration changes of goldfish do not necessarily mean that there is a change in health. The cause may be dietary or it may be due to events beyond the control of the aquarist. Patches of black or silver may develop and disappear without obvious causes in goldfish.

GOLDFISH PARASITES

Surface parasites, some of which are large enough to be easily seen whilst others are microscopic in size, are not always easy to deal with, but organisms living inside the goldfish can scarcely be reached at all. The fish usually betray the presence of skin parasites by their efforts to remove the irritation as they flick and roll their bodies against the sand or water plants.

Gill worms (*Gyrodactylus* and *Dactylogyrus*) are very common parasites which are only just visible to the eye. They do not restrict themselves to the gills, but spread all over the body surface. When present in breeding tanks they cause the deaths of many fry, but usually they only weaken the adult fish and cause them to look in poor shape. Heavily infected fish may show patches of blood in the skin and greyish areas on their bodies. The worms can leave the fish and swim free in the water so that overcrowded tanks suit them best of all.

Treatment of the fish is carried out as follows: While the fish is held in a net it is fully immersed in a bowl containing a quart of water into which one teaspoonful of Dettol has been stirred. After only fifteen seconds in this solution the fish is taken out and placed at once in a large bowl of clean water. After an interval of one day the treatment is repeated. The infected aquarium must be dismantled and disinfected, and all nets used for the fish must also be treated.

White spot disease is the result of infection with a microscopic ciliated protozoan known as *Ichthyophthirius*, and it produces pin-head-sized white blisters over the fins and body of the fish. It is not common in goldfish, but is a troublesome disease to get rid of, since in the parasitic life cycle exists a resistant encysted stage away from the fish. This necessitates thoroughly cleaning the aquarium. The fish are placed in water to which has been added sufficient quinine sulphate solution to give a concentration of three grains to the gallon. This solution is renewed every other day until the spots disappear.

Anchor worms *(Lernæa)* may be seen to protrude from small pimple-like swellings on the skin, one worm to each pimple, and the worms retract into the skin if disturbed. The fish must be netted, and whilst it is held out of water the spots are dabbed with cotton wool soaked in bleaching solution of household ammonia to kill the worms, strict care being taken to see that the chemicals are not spread over the body of the fish or on to the gills.

Fish lice *(Argulus)* appear as greyish-green flat, round plates about an eighth of an inch across, and they can be picked off the fish with forceps whilst it is held in a net. The parasite can live for about three days in the absence of a fish host, and it will lay numerous eggs in rows on the glass of aquaria.

Leeches seen attached to goldfish can be removed without damaging the fish by transferring it to a strong solution of salt in water for a short time (four tablespoons of salt to the gallon).

DISINFECTION OF PONDS AND AQUARIA

Adequate disinfection of ponds and aquaria contaminated by disease organisms can only be done chemically in the absence of the fish, and the treatment, to be efficacious, may also kill the water plants. These can harbour the eggs or resistant stages of the parasites, however, so it is not worth worrying about their loss. The most convenient sterilizing agent is bleaching powder (chloride of lime), and a concentration of twenty parts of chlorine per million is given by dissolving an ounce of the powder for every 100 gallons of water in a pond, or by dissolving a level teaspoonful of the powder in every ten gallons of water in an aquarium. Do not add the chemical in sunlight, for this expedites removal of the chlorine. After twenty-four hours the solution is discarded and the aquarium or pond is cleaned out before restocking.

Common causes of poisoning of goldfish include contamination of the water with metals or lime. The most toxic metal is copper (0·5 parts per million of copper sulphate is lethal to goldfish), so that copper or brass objects should not be used in ponds or aquaria. The risk of poisoning from, say, copper piping, is greater in soft than in hard waters. Lime emerges from the cement in newly laid concrete, and this should not be brought into contact with water in which fishes are to be kept unless it has been thoroughly washed or given a protective coating.

Plastics are mostly non-poisonous to fish, and there are several aquarium accessories made from perspex; cellulose acetate is an exception to the general rule, however. This sometimes contains diethyl phthalate, and although only slightly soluble in water, this chemical is rapidly fatal to goldfish and plants.

CHAPTER 8

SHOWS AND SHOWING
by
A. BOARDER

DURING the past forty years or so many shows have been held in this country, but it is safe to say that many more have been held since 1946 than in the twenty years preceding that time. This is not to be wondered at when one considers the great increase in the numbers of aquarists' societies since 1946. Whether the number of shows held each year will increase at a proportionate rate in the coming years is a matter for conjecture. My own view is that saturation point has already been reached. Many societies are finding that the expense incurred in running an open show does not bring satisfactory returns. By combining the show with an event staged by another type of society, such as a local cage birds or horticultural society, some societies have found that these expenses are reduced.

There is more than one type of show held, and intending exhibitors should make sure that a show in which they wish to compete is open to them. The Open Show, as its name implies, is open to anyone. The Club Show is open usually to club members only, while an Inter-Club Show is open to members of those clubs participating in such joint action. Besides holding annual shows many societies hold table shows at their meetings, and a schedule is generally prepared to provide that most of the recognized types of fish will have a class in at least one of the shows. Points are often awarded at these table shows, and the members with most points at the end of the season receive a cup or similar award.

Club shows serve a very useful purpose in letting the exhibitor see how his fish compares with others from the society. I am of the opinion that it is very unwise for anyone to enter a fish in an open show unless the fish has already won an award in a Club

84

Show. Once he has seen his fish competing with others of the same type at a Club Show the aquarist can far more easily form an idea as to whether the fish is worth entering for open competition. There is little chance of a bad-type fish winning at a big show, and its entry only adds to the work of the judges unnecessarily.

It is usual for types of goldfish to be provided with a class at practically every open show. There are so many different types of goldfish that it is not possible at most shows to allot a separate class for each distinct variety. At some open shows the emphasis is definitely on tropical fish and the goldfish has to be content with one class or two. At most of the leading shows which have been held during the past seven years there has been a class for the common goldfish, one for shubunkins, one for veiltails and moors, and one for 'A.O.V. goldfish'. This A.O.V. means any other variety not included in the schedule.

Some shows have a class for the London shubunkin as well as the Bristol, and others have one for the fantail. I have never yet seen a complete schedule for the eight distinct types of goldfish at any one show, and the different varieties have to fight it out among themselves. This is a very unsatisfactory method, for how can one assess the value of a fantail even if it has won a first prize when it was only competing against veiltails, moors, shubunkins and sometimes other types as well? So many shows are held annually that it should be easy with a little co-operation to be able to provide separate classes for each of the distinct types among the shows each year within certain areas.

F.B.A.S. STANDARDS FOR JUDGING

At practically all the leading shows held in the British Isles the fish are judged according to the standards which have been introduced by the Federation of British Aquatic Societies. Their findings have been published in a booklet which can be obtained from the Federation. All exhibitors should be in possession of this booklet as it shows quite plainly what properties are required in a specific type and how the points are awarded.

The standards in the F.B.A.S. booklet were only arrived at after careful thought by a group of judges and specialists, working from actual fish and photographs, and while it is not suggested that they are the last word, they are at least a very useful guide and ones to which it is possible to work fairly easily during judging. There have been one or two attempts by various societies to form their own standards, but apart from their being able to make their own conditions at their individual shows, they are not likely to be accepted by the majority of aquarists throughout the country.

Aquarists may wonder how they can tell whether their fish are of sufficient standard of excellence to warrant their being exhibited. The booklet mentioned will help a lot, but it is better to enlist the help of a recognized specialist in the particular type in question. If one belongs to a club it is fairly easy to become acquainted with all the recognized types and to see them in competition at club shows. Some aquarists are unfortunate in that they do not reside within easy distance of a club, and they are the ones who will find it a little more difficult to assess the worth of their fish. A visit to a well-known show will be well worthwhile, and if one attends with a mental picture of the fish it is planned to exhibit, it is possible to make comparisons with the winners seen.

Although an aquarist may have a very good idea of the correct appearance of a type of fish, it is quite possible to rear fish and to be with them so much that a fault may not be noticeable to the owner while it would be immediately so to an outsider. In these days of aquarist magazines and frequent shows it should be easy for anyone to know whether his fish is worth exhibiting or not, but some of the specimens seen at some shows make one wonder whether their owners have ever seen a decent fish.

Once you have made up your mind that you have one or two fish which you consider worth showing there are several things you must do. If you are a member of an aquarist club it will be fairly easy for you to learn the ropes, but if you are not you will have to watch for advertisements in *The Aquarist* monthly magazine announcing forthcoming shows. When you have found a show at which you would like to exhibit, send at once to the show secretary for a schedule. Examine this very carefully to see if there is a class for your actual type, and if not make sure that it can go in one of the others.

I have beside me a schedule for probably the largest annual open show held in London each year. It is that for June, 1953, and reads, for coldwater entries: Class 1. Common goldfish; Class 2. Bristol shubunkin; Class 3. London shubunkin; Class 4. Fantails; Class 5. Veiltails and moors; Class 6. Orandas and lionheads; Class 7. British coldwater fishes; Class 8. Foreign coldwater fishes—and so on to the tropicals. It will be seen that although the London shubunkin has been given a separate class there is no class for the comet or celestial. As there is no class for A.O.V. fancy goldfish, these two varieties are not catered for and so could not be shown.

So, read your schedule carefully, and when you have made up your mind which classes you wish to enter, fill in the form correctly and send it in as soon as possible with the entrance fees. Some schedules specify that only one entry must be made in each class, but this is a bad rule as it prevents the specialist breeder from showing two or three fish of his breeding so that an independent judge can place them in their winning order. This is a most important point, as I have already stated how one can get so used to a fish whilst rearing it that small faults may be overlooked. The specialist breeder wants to know his best fish from an exhibition point of view so that only the best types are bred from.

TRAINING FOR SHOWING

Once the schedules are sent off you must start preparing the fish for the show bench. Some fish are natural performers in a show tank, while others will skulk at the bottom and give the judge no chance of seeing their best points. By constantly placing a fish in a tank similar to a show tank and getting it used to company, it is possible to get an ordinary pond fish quite accustomed to the upset of changed quarters well before the time of the show. For large goldfish, tanks as large as twenty-four inches by twelve inches by twelve inches may be used, but usually they will be not more than about twelve inches by eight inches by eight inches. Some schedules ask for the size of the fish, and if this is filled in correctly it may help to save your six-inch fish from being placed in a small tank while another fish not half the size in the same class may have a tank twice as big.

You must also watch the feeding of the fish prior to the actual show. Give as much live food as possible, and if you have any *Daphnia* see that as soon as the fish is put into your training tank a few *Daphnia* are added. The fish will get to expect this treat, and once it is put in the show tank will swim about looking for more, which, not being there, will keep it alert for the judging.

Meanwhile you should have received from the show secretary your exhibition tank numbers. The schedule will show the time when all exhibits must be in their tanks and all exhibitors cleared from the hall ready for judging. This time is the dead-line and has to be conformed with. It should never be possible for fish to be placed in their show tanks in the presence of the judges.

TRANSPORTING THE FISH

If you live within fairly easy reach of the show it is better to take the fish yourself. If the show is at a distance you will have to send the fish by rail, unless you know someone who is going and can take your fish for you. Most shows allow the fish to be put in their tanks overnight, and give a time limit for the morning prior to the actual judging. I have always preferred to take my fish to shows in the mornings so that they do not have to be in the tanks too long. On the other hand, if a fish has not been well trained it would be as well to put it in the tank overnight so that it could settle down. If you have to send by rail make sure that arrangements have been made for the reception at the other end. Stewards are as a rule appointed to see to this problem. See that the fish can is sound and has no leak. Do not put too much water in it; less than half full is sufficient. Clearly label the can and place a red 'Live Stock' label on too. Take it to the railway station, where you will have the can weighed and will be required to fill in a couple of forms. It is sometimes possible to see the fish actually put on the train, and this is a great help.

Should you be taking the fish yourself you may find that when you reach the exhibition hall utter confusion will meet your eye. It is not often that a show can be run without this last-minute rush and apparent muddle. This is not always the promoters' fault, as the hall may not have been available until almost the last minute. Go to the show secretary's table and report to him. He will give you the tank numbers if they have not been sent before. A steward will show you the class, and you then find your tank. See that there is no mistake as to tank numbers. Sometimes you find a fish already in the tank which should be yours, and enquiries will show that the class number has been mistaken for the tank number.

The tanks are usually filled with water, but if this is not to your liking it can be emptied and re-filled. Compare the temperature of the water in the tank with that of the carrying can. Some stewards are so 'tropical-minded' that they keep on two large wattage electric lamps for hours over a coldwater tank until the temperature of the water is up to 85° F. in the winter, and fish are supposed to be placed therein having come from an open pond with a temperature in the region of 40° F. If the show is held in the summer the opposite may be the case. The tank may have been recently filled from the main with icy water, while the can may have warmed up over 70° F. If you do not check the temperature the fish may get such a shock and it may so upset them as to cause them to fold up at the bottom with little chance of getting that award card.

When placing fish from a can into the tank I advise that the hand is used instead of a net. With care and practice it is possible to handle a goldfish much more safely with the hands than with a net. Nets can cause split fins or other damage. Once the fish are all in their correct tanks, see that your can is properly labelled and hand it in for safe storage until it is needed.

FISH JUDGING

You will then leave the show and your fish to the tender, or otherwise, mercies of the judge. He may deal with all or a few of the classes according to the size of the show. The numbers in the class will determine the length and difficulty of his task. If the class is of thirty or more fish it will be impossible for him to 'point up' all the fish. He will probably look over all the fish in the one class he is starting with and note down all those which he considers to be worth pointing. He may find six or eight really good ones, or he may have a job to find a couple. The latter position is far more difficult for him, as although it is comparatively easy to pick out excellent types it is very hard to find winners among a poor lot. This is when your preliminary training may bring profits. The alert fish moving about with all the fins spread is more likely to catch the eye of the judge than the fish which is huddled up on the bottom of the tank with all the fins folded.

When pointing the fish the judge will look for special points according to the type in the class. If the class is for shubunkins he will look first for the required colours, as this feature receives the most points. For fishes like veiltails and fantails he will pay special attention to the tails, and so on. In most of the varieties very few points are allotted for the actual condition of the fish; the number varies according to the type, but it makes a great deal of difference for a fish if it is so healthy and vigorous that its brightness stands out and so shows off not only all the fins but the colour as well. It can be seen from this that the busy judge cannot spend minutes waiting for a particular fish to wake and show off its good points. This is often the reason why some fish win at one show and fail to get an award in another.

It is quite possible that the judge will soon spot a bad fault in a fish such as a single anal fin where two are required, and in fact when competition is keen it may mean that he has deliberately to look for slight faults to make up his mind about the winning fish. As a rule the fish with the highest points is the winner, but this is not always so. In large classes I have known more than one fish in a class to be awarded the same number of points; then another examination is necessary to pick the actual winner. If only the judge could move the tanks around into winning positions for comparisons, as is done with cage birds, how simple it would all be. Instead of this the judge may have to run round the other side of the staging to compare the first with the second and then back again for the others!

When you have curbed your impatience until the judging has been completed you will at last know your fate. Don't expect too much and then you will not be so disappointed if success has not come your way. It may be possible to see the judge and get some valuable tips from him as to the worth of your fish. If this is possible I consider it to be well worth while as you may learn a lot. In time you will be able, when placing your fish in their tanks, to place the awards yourself, and when this happy state arrives you are well on the road to success on the show bench. It is a good plan after you have had a quick look round to make some notes not only of the winning owners but also the winning fish. There may be a fish on show which has the very desirable point which your own strain requires, and you may be able to get some fresh stock or make exchanges to the advantage of your stock in future breeding seasons. It is often possible to gain much useful information during discussion by the actual exhibits, as reference to the fish on show will help solve many more difficulties than could be the case were the fish not there.

AFTER THE SHOW

No fish may be removed from the show until a given time, except for exceptional circumstances. Also, it is usual for a rule to be made that no fish may be taken without there being an attendant present. Take care when removing the fish from the tank that the water in the can is about the same temperature as that in the tank to avoid shocks. Once the fish are home again it is a good plan to keep the exhibits by themselves for a few days. Remember that it is a bit of a shock for a goldfish to spend three or more days in a small show tank and then be dumped back into a cold open pond. Let the temperatures of the water reach about the same level and return the fish to the pond when it shows no ill-effects. I find that the exhibition of fish even during the breeding season does no apparent harm to my fish as long as I use average care with them.

Once a fish has gained a first or even a second prize with keen competition at a good class show, the value of it has been enhanced considerably. A winner can fetch say ten pounds against fifty pence or so for a good fish not actually a winner. The owner may not wish to part with it, however, as it will be of much more value as a breeder. There is no doubt that you are far more likely to produce good fish from a good prize-winning strain than from a nondescript type.

The value of open shows cannot be over-emphasized. As with

other kinds of animal life, such as dogs, cats, rabbits and cage birds, it is only by frequent shows that the standards can be kept high. There would be no incentives to keep up the standards of the numerous types of dogs were it not for the shows. With fancy goldfish, if there were no shows the specialist breeder would not be able to get experienced judges' opinions of the fish and the public would be unable to see how a good type should appear.

With the idea of improving all the types of goldfish I consider that the Federation of British Aquatic Societies should do all possible to encourage societies to arrange at their annual shows for classes for *all* the main types. The usual cry of the show promoters when asked why more classes are not provided is that they cannot afford the prizes. I feel sure that all true enthusiasts who are breeding particular strains would willingly forgo the prize money as long as they could place their fish in competition among others of the same variety. Without the shows the quality of the fancy goldfish must deteriorate, and this would be a very sad day for all those who have spent so much time and thought producing special strains.

A few 'don'ts' in conclusion. *Don't* expect to exhibit a runt and win with it in an open show. *Don't* show a fish which is not in good condition. If you are a club member *don't* criticize a show when all you have done towards it is to stand with your hands in your pockets while others do all the work. *Don't* leave your fish at home and then tell everyone at the show that you have far better fish there than any of the winners. *Don't* blame the show stewards for something which has gone wrong when care on your own part could have avoided the trouble. If you get a 'first' at a club table show, *don't* go about boasting of your success; wait until you can win in the open or get a special award for the 'best fish in the show'.

APPENDIX

POND CONSTRUCTION

AUTUMN is the time to undertake pond construction work. Weather conditions are then most suitable for concreting, and the pond can be prepared for stocking well before the following spring. Either a formal or an informal design may be decided upon, and a detailed plan with dimensions should be prepared. Suitable measurements for a small rectangular garden pond are six feet by five feet, with the deepest part about two feet six inches. An area slightly larger (*i.e.,* seven feet by six feet) is marked on the proposed pond site with pegs and lengths of string and the soil is removed to depths about six inches more than those indicated on the plan. The bottom can slope from one end to the other to provide varying depths, or ledges can be made to form the shallower parts around a central deep region. At the deepest part drainage pipes can be laid to meet a nearby sump or main drain, to facilitate emptying the pond. Large stones and brick rubble rammed into the earth bottom and sides will strengthen them and form good concreting surfaces.

Concrete Mixing.—Materials required for concrete mixing are: cement (one part), builder's sand (Class A fine aggregate —two parts) and shingle (three parts). These proportions are by volume, not by weight; a bucket can be used to measure out the amounts, sufficient concrete being mixed at a time to give a mass capable of being placed in position within an hour. Mix the materials on a clean hard surface with a spade. Cement and sand are first mixed, then the shingle is added and the whole mixed again. Water is sprinkled on this and mixing is continued until an evenly coloured and dispersed mass is obtained. Approximately half a bucket of water for each bucket of sand is necessary. If coloured concrete is desired pigments can be added to the mix, or cement of the chosen colour ordered. For each square yard of the pond's inner surface to be concreted four inches to six inches thick there is required eighty-three pounds of cement, one and three-quarter cubic feet of sand and two and three-quarter cubic feet of shingle. The pond bottom is laid first, smoothed over with a trowel, and then left to harden.

Placing Concrete at the Sides.—Some old timbers and planking are needed to form temporary walls about five inches away from the earth sides. This 'shuttering' is fixed rigidly in position when the bottom is hard, and fresh concrete is shovelled into the space behind it and compacted with the spade. Level the top edges carefully with a spirit level on a board so that all the walls are the same height. After about a week the shuttering is removed and the concrete surface smoothed over by using a mixture of one part cement to two parts of sand with water. During warm, dry weather all concrete must be kept damp by covering it with wet sacks during the period allowed for hardening. A pond surround of concrete slabs or paving stones, to overlap the top edges of the walls, can be cemented in position as a final procedure.

Preparing the Pond.—Fill the newly concreted pond with water and allow it to remain filled for at least a fortnight. Then empty it and scrub the sides and bottom with a hard brush before refilling with water for a further soaking period of two weeks. Repeat the emptying, scrubbing and soaking procedure at least three more times. This is an essential operation to free the new concrete from lime which would otherwise render the pond unfit for fish and plants. An alternative procedure is to seal in the lime with coats of bituminous paint (this needs a less lengthy soaking in water to prepare it for the fish) or coats of water glass (sodium silicate) dissolved in water. Using commercial phosphoric acid to make the water of the new pond acid (checked with litmus paper) will neutralize lime from the concrete. This last method reduces the time needed to prepare the pond, but the acid solution must be removed after a few days' soaking, and the pond needs rinsing to be ready for stocking.

Pond Capacities.—Gallon capacity of rectangular ponds is found by multiplying together the length, width and average depth (all in feet), and further multiplication of the product by six and a quarter. For circular ponds the diameter in feet is squared and multiplied by the depth in feet times 4·9, to give the capacity in gallons.

BOOKS FOR FURTHER READING

The Goldfish, by G. F. Hervey and J. Hems (Batchworth; London, 1948).

The Cult of the Goldfish, by T. C. Roughley (Angus and Robertson; London, 1949).

Aquariums, by Anthony Evans (Foyles Handbooks; London, 1951).

Water Gardening, by Frances Perry (Country Life; London, 1947).

Show Standards for Cultivated Fishes (Federation of British Aquatic Societies; London, 1947).

Periodical: *Pet Fish Monthly* (London).

Garden Ponds, by A. Boarder (Foyles).

AQUARIUM SOCIETIES

THE address of the society of aquarium-keepers nearest to any particular locality in Britain will be supplied on request (accompanied by a self-addressed envelope) from *Pet Fish Monthly*, 554 Garratt Lane, London, S.W.17.